INTRODUCTORY NOTES

Covered in this Review are the major activities of the various ministries, commissions, directorates, offices and administrations under the Executive *Yuan* (the Cabinet) of the Republic of China and the performance thereof over the past years.

Information included herein was obtained directly from the various authorities concerned.

Depending on the specific needs in the different cases, either calendar years or fiscal years are used in compilation of the statistical data.

A part of the data for 1973 are preliminary estimates and are subject to revision next year.

This review is published both in Chinese and English editions.

CONTENTS

GOVERNMENT ORGANIZATION

AT END OF 1973

NATIONAL SECURITY COUNCIL

PRESIDENT

VICE PRESIDENT

THE PRESIDENTIAL OFFICE

EXAMINATION YUAN
- MINISTRY OF PERSONNEL
- MINISTRY OF EXAMINATION

JUDICIAL YUAN
- COMMITTEE ON THE DISCIPLINE OF PUBLIC FUNCTIONARIES
- ADMINISTRATIVE COURT
- SUPREME COURT

EXECUTIVE YUAN
- SPECIAL COMMISSIONS
- GOVERNMENT INFORMATION OFFICE
- PERSONNEL ADMINISTRATION OFFICE
- DIRECTORATE GENERAL OF BUDGET ACCOUNTING AND STATISTICS
- SECRETARIAT
- NATIONAL HEALTH ADININISTRATION
- OVERSEAS CHINESE AFFAIRS COMMISSION
- MONGOLIAN AND TIBETAN COMMISSION
- MINISTRY OF COMMUNICATIONS
- MINISTRY OF ECONOMIC AFFAIRS
- MINISTRY OF JUSTICE
- MINISTRY OF EDUCATION
- MINISTRY OF FINANCE
- MINISTRY OF NATIONAL DEFENSE
- MINISTRY OF FOREIGN AFFAIRS
- MINISTRY OF THE INTERIOR

CONTROL YUAN
- MINISTRY OF AUDIT
- COMMITTEES

LEGISLATIVE YUAN
- COMMITTEES

NATIONAL ASSEMBLY

Land utilization and major construction projects in the Taiwan area

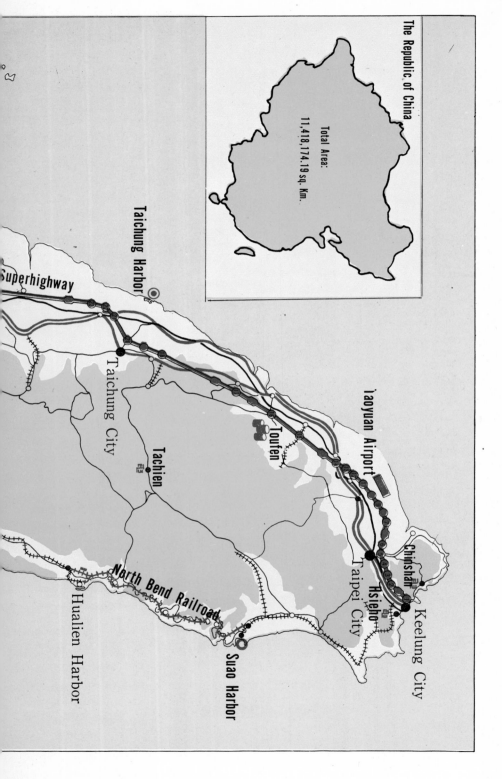

The Republic of China

Total Area:
11,418,174.19 sq. Km.

Superhighway

Taichung Harbor

Taichung City

Tachien

Toufen

Taoyuan Airport

Chinshan

Keelung City

Hsieho

Taipei City

North Bend Railroad

Hualien Harbor

Suao Harbor

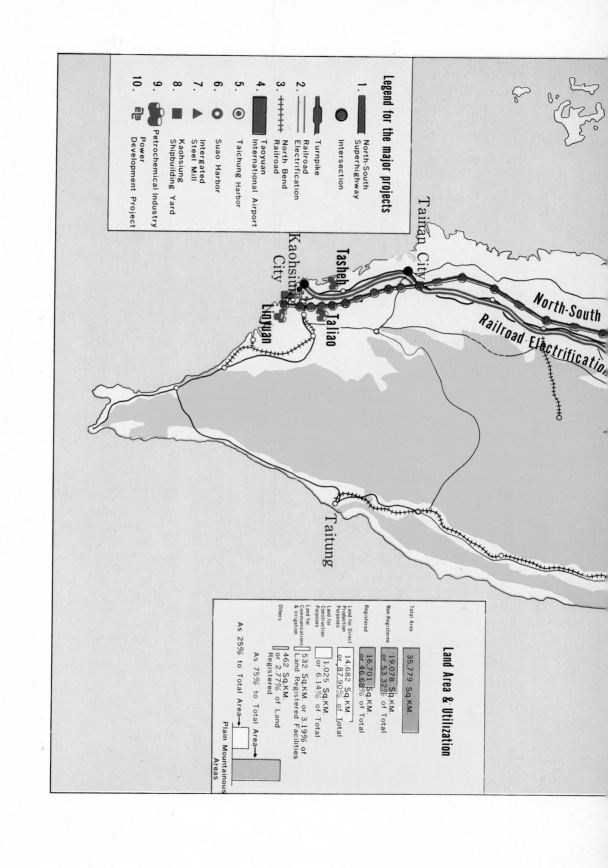

Legend for the major projects

1. ▬ North-South
   Superhighway
   ● Intersection
2. ▬ Turnpike
3. ┼┼┼┼┼ North Bend
   Railroad
   ▬ Railroad
   Electrification
4. ▬ Taoyuan
   International Airport
5. ◉ Taichung Harbor
6. ○ Suao Harbor
7. ▶ Intergated
   Steel Mill
8. ■ Kaohsiung
   Shipbuilding Yard
9. ⬛ Petrochemical Industry
10. 🏭 Power
    Development Project

Tainan City

Kaohsiung
City

Tasheh

Taliao

Linyuan

North-South

Railroad Electrification

Taitung

Land Area & Utilization

Total Area		35,779 Sq.KM.
Non-Registered		19,078 Sq.KM. or 53.32% of Total
Registered		16,701 Sq.KM. or 46.68% of Total
Land for Direct Production Purposes		14,682 Sq.KM. or 87.90% of Total
Land for Construction Purposes		1,025 Sq.KM. or 6.14% of Total
Land for Communications & Irrigation		532 Sq.KM. or 3.19% of Land Registered Facilities
Others		462 Sq.KM. or 2.77% of Land Registered

As 25% to Total Area →
As 75% to Total Area →

Plain Areas
Mountainous Areas

MUNICIPAL GOVERNMENT UNDER DIRECT JURISDICTION OF THE EXECUTIVE YUAN

AFFILIATED AGENCIES

DEPARTMENT OF PERSONNEL

DEPARTMENT OF ACCOUNTING AND STATISTICS

DEPARTMENT OF INFORMATION

SECRETARIAT

LAND ADMINISTRATION

DEPARTMENT OF ENVIRONMENTAL CLEANING

BUREAU OF HEALTH

POLICE BUREAU

BUREAU OF SOCIAL AFFAIRS

BUREAU OF ENGINEERING

BUREAU OF RECONSTRUCTION

BUREAU OF EDUCATION

BUREAU OF FINANCE

BUREAU OF CIVIL AFFAIRS

CITY GOVERNMENT

DISTRICT OFFICE

AFFILIATED AGENCIES

OTHER SUBORDINATE AGENCIES

BUREAU OF HEALTH

POLICE BUREAU

TAX BUREAU

URBAN DISTRICT OFFICE

OFFICE OF PERSONNEL

OFFICE OF ACCOUTING AND STATISTICS

SECRETARIAT

PROVINCIAL GOVERNMENT

AFFILIATED AGENCIES

DEPARTMENT OF PERSONNEL

DEPARTMENT OF ACCOUNTING AND STATISTICS

SECRETARIAT

FOOD BUREAU

DEPARTMENT OF INFORMATION

HEALTH DEPARTMENT

DEPARIMENT OF COMMUNICATIONS

POLICE DEPARTMENT

DEPARTMENT OF SOCIAL AFFAIRS

DEPARTMENT OF AGRICULTURE AND FORESTRY

DEPARTMENT OF RECONSTRUCTION

DEPARTMENT OF EDUCATION

DEPARTMENT OF FINANCE

DEPARTMENT OF CIVIL AFFAIRS

COUNTY (ADMINISTRATION) GOVERMNENT

OFFICE OF COOPERATIVES

OFFICE OF INFORMATION

SECTION OF CONSCRIPTION

SECTION OF LAND ADMINISTRATION

SECTION OF SOCIAL AFFAIRS

BUREAU OF RECONSTRUCTION

BUREAU (SECTION) OF EDUCTION

BUREAU (SECTION) OF FINANCE

BUREAU OF CIVIL AFFARIS

BOROUGH DISTRICT OR TOWN OFFICE

THE PRESENT GOVERNMENT HIERARCHY

SYSTEM OF GOVERNMENT

Founded in 1911, the Republic of China was the first republic to come into existence in Asia. The government system is framed after the doctrine of Dr. Sun Yat-sen, father of the Republic. It has the following four characteristic features:

Supreme authority in the hands of the people

The supreme authority of the nation, which is a republic of the people, by the people and for the people, is in the hands of the whole body of citizens.

Division of political and administrative powers

Pursuant to Dr. Sun's doctrine, the nation's political authority has been divided into political and administrative powers. The former is vested in the National Assembly while the latter is exercised by the President and the Central Government.

The political power, in fact, is the popular power exercised on behalf of the people by the National Assembly, which is therefore empowered to elect and recall the President and the Vice President and to introduce new legislation as well as to vote on an existing law to supercede or overrule it.

Separation of five administrative powers

The five-power theory was created by Dr. Sun by combining the three Western powers of legislation, execution and judicature with the two traditional Chinese powers of examination and control.

Balance of powers between the central and the local governments

The division of authority between the central and the local governments is based on the principle of balance of power. Matters that are national in nature all fall under the jurisdiction of the Central Government; and those that should be handled differently in different contexts, under the jurisdiction of local governments.

ORGANIZATION OF GOVERNMENT

The Central Government is composed of the Presidential Office, the President's staff and directly subordinate organizations and the five government branches; namely, the Executive, Legislative, Judicial, Examination and Control *Yuan*. The local governments are: the provincial and special municipality governments, *hsien* (county) and *shih* (city) governments and *hsiang* and *chen* (township) governments.

Central Government

The President

The President and the Vice President are elected by the National Assembly for a term of six years.

As head of the State, the President represents the nation in foreign relations, and exercises the powers of concluding treaties, declaring war and making peace in accordance with the provisions of the Constitution of the Republic of China. The President is the supreme commander of the land, sea, and air forces of the country, and exercises, in accordance with law, the powers of promulgating laws, issuing mandates, appointing and removing civil and military officers, conferring honors and decorations, declaring martial law, and granting amnesties, pardons, commutation of sentences and restitution of civil rights.

THE PRESIDENT'S STAFF ORGANIZATIONS

Title	Functions
Senior Advisors	To make recommendations to the President on major policies concerning affairs of the State and stand ready for consultation by the President.
Secretary-General	To take general charge of the affairs of the Presidential Office under the President's guidance. (The Secretary-General is assisted by a Deputy Secretary-General).
Personal Chief of Staff to the President	To attend to matters concerning military affairs under the President's guidance.
National Policy Advisory Committee	To make recommendations to the President on matters relating to national reconstruction.
Planning Commission for the Recovery of the Mainland	To study and plan for the recovery of the Chinese mainland.

ORGANIZATIONS IMMEDIATELY SUBORDINATE TO THE PRESIDENT

Title	Functions
Academia Sinica	To conduct scientific research and provide guidance for academic studies. (The academy is the highest research institute in the Republic of China.)
Academia Historica	To compile the history of the Republic of China.

Central Bank of China	A national bank authorized by the Government to issue notes, operate as the national treasury, and raise funds from both domestic and international sources.
National Security Council	(a) To lay down the general plan and overall guidelines for resources mobilization for the suppression of the Communist rebellion; (b) to shape national defense policy; (c) to formulate guidelines for national reconstruction and science development; (d) to plan and provide guidance for undertaking of a total war; (e) to make decisions on general mobilization; (f) to lay out schemes for administering of affairs in war areas; and (g) to take up other problems relating to resources mobilization for suppression of Communist rebellion and matters assigned to it by the President for its study and comment.

The Five Yuan

The Executive Yuan: The Executive *Yuan*, the highest administrative organ of the State, has a president, a vice president, heads of a number of ministries and commissions, and several ministers without portfolio. The president of the *Yuan* is nominated and, with the consent of the Legislative *Yuan*, appointed by the President of the Republic. The ministers and heads of commissions are appointed by the President of the Republic upon the recommendation of the president of the *Yuan*. The president of the *Yuan* is in overall charge of the affairs of his office and supervises the operations of its subordinate agencies. The *Yuan* has an Executive Council composed of the entire members of the *Yuan* with the president of the *Yuan* as its chairman. The Council is responsible for discussion and finalization of statutory or budgetary bills and bills concerning martial law, general amnesty, declaration of war, conclusion of peace or treaties and other important matters to be submitted to the Legislative *Yuan*, as well as matters that are of concern to more than one Ministry and Commission.

The Legislative Yuan: It is the highest legislative organ of the State and is composed of legislators elected by the people. It exercises legislative power on behalf of the people to pass bills, statutes, and budgets, and consider bills concerning the enforcement of martial law, general amnesty, declaration of war and conclusion of peace and to approve treaties and other important matters of the nation. It has a president and a vice president elected by and from among the legislators. The president of the *Yuan* takes overall charge of its affairs and serves as the chairman at legislative meetings. In the Legislative *Yuan* there are a number of committees to deal with various aspects of public affairs.

The Judicial *Yuan:* The highest judicial organ of the State, the Judicial *Yuan* has charge of last instance of civil, criminal and administrative cases and of cases concerning the discipline of public functionaries. It has a president, a vice president and a council of 17 grand justices, who are nominated and, with the consent of the Control *Yuan,* appointed by the President of the Republic. The council of grand justices, which is chaired by the president of the *Yuan*, is responsible for interpretation of the Constitution, laws and mandates. Under the *Yuan* are the Supreme Court, the Administrative Court and the Committee on Discipline of Public Functionaries. The president of the *Yuan* takes overall charge of its affairs and suprevises its subordinate organizations.

The Examination *Yuan:* The Examination *Yuan,* the highest examination organ of the State, handles such aspects of personnel administration as examination, selection, appointment, performance evaluation, establishment of pay scales, promotion, service protection, awards, compensation, retirement and pensions. It has a president, a vice-president and a number of members to be nominated and, with the consent of the Control *Yuan,* appointed by the President of the Republic. The president of the *Yuan* takes overall charge of its affairs and serves as the chairman at meetings. Under the *Yuan,* there are the Ministry of Examination and Ministry of Personnel.

The Control *Yuan:* It is the highest control organ of the State and is composed of members elected by provincial assemblies and municipal councils, the local councils of Mongolia and Tibet, and Chinese citizens residing abroad. It exercises the power of consent, impeachment, censure and audit. It has a president and a vice-president elected by and from among its members. The president of the *Yuan* takes overall charge of its affairs and serves as the chairman at meetings. It may establish various committees. Under the *Yuan* there is a Ministry of Audit.

MINISTRIES & COMMISSIONS

Under the Executive *Yuan*

Title	Functions
Ministry of the Interior	Domestic Administrative affairs
Ministry of Foreign Affairs	International negotiations and all matters pertaining to Chinese nationals residing abroad, alien residents in China and commercial affairs relating to aliens.
Ministry of National Defense	Planning and execution of national defense program and military installations.
Ministry of Finance	Fiscal administration.
Ministry of Education	Academic and educational affairs.
Ministry of Justice	Judicial administrative affairs.
Ministry of Economic Affairs	Economic administration affairs and economic development.
Ministry of Communications	Planning, construction, control and operation of railways, highways, tele-communication, post office and navigation systems, and supervision of public and private communication enterprises.
Mongolian and Tibetan Affairs Commission	Matters concerning Mongolia and Tibet
Overseas Chinese Affairs Commission	Overseas Chinese affairs administration and assistance to overseas Chinese enterprises.
(Heads of Ministries and Commissions are ex-officio members of the Executive Council)	
National Health Administration	Health and drug administration.

Local Government

There is a provincial government in each province and a municipal government in each special municipality directly under the jurisdiction of the Executive *Yuan*. Under a province there are *hsien* (counties) and *shih* (cities) with respective *hsien* or *shih* governments; under a *hsien* (county) there are *hsiang*, *chen* or townships with their respective offices.

ELECTIONS TO PUBLIC OFFICES

ELECTION OF REPRESENTATIVES TO THE CENTRAL GOVERNMENT

The 1969 election

Following the jurisdictional re-adjustment in the Taiwan area (Taipei City was made a special municipality directly under the jurisdiction of the Executive *Yuan* in July 1968), special elections of representatives to the Central Government in accordance with the Temporary Provisions of the Constitution were held in Taiwan Province and Taipei City on December 12 and December 29, 1969 respectively, whereby 15 National Assembly Delegates, 11 Legislators and two Control *Yuan* Members were elected.

The 1972 election

To increase the efficiency of the nation's legislature, another national level election was held among the residents of the Taiwan area, Kinmen and Matsu, and Chinese living elsewhere in the Free World, with the result that 53 National Assembly Delegates, 51 Legislators and 10 Control *Yuan* Members were elected.

All the newly elected took their offices and have since been performing their duties at the various parliamentary organs.

SELF-GOVERNMENT IN TAIWAN

Taipei City Councilmen

In July 1968 the City of Taipei was elevated to the status of a special municipality and came directly under the jurisdiction of the Executive *Yuan*. Members of the First Post-Elevation Taipei City Council were elected in a popular election. Their tenure began on December 25, 1969 and ended on December 25, 1973. A second Taipei City Council was elected in 1973, with the tenure of its members to last from December 25, 1973 to December 25, 1977. The Taipei City Council has the functions of examining and deciding on city legislation, budget estimates and final statements submitted by the Taipei City Government.

Provincial Assembly Members

The First Taiwan Provisional Provincial Assembly was instituted in November 1951 through indirect election by the members of the various county and city councils. The tenure of the members was two years. Beginning with the Second Provisional Provincial Assembly, the tenure was extended from two to three years. Since then, the members have been elected from the counties and cities through popular vote. In April 1959, the First Taiwan Provincial Assembly was formally inaugurated. Since April 1963, the tenure of the members has been extended to four years. The present Assembly is the fifth one—or the seventh counting from the First Provisional Assembly. The average turnout of voters in the assembly members election was 73.73%.

The Provincial Assembly has the function of examining and deciding on provincial legislation, budget estimates and final statements submitted by the Provincial Government.

County and City Councilmen

Since July 1950, all Councilmen have been elected directly by popular vote. For the First and Second Councils, the tenure was only two years. The tenure was extended to three years for the Third, Fourth and Fifth Councils. Beginning with the Sixth Council, it was further extended to four years. The average turnout in the past elections was about 78.04%. The functions of county and city councils include examination and passing of ordinances concerning self-government,, special

regulations applicable to their respective districts, and budget estimates and final statements submitted by the county and city governments.

Magistrates and Mayors

Since October 1950, with the introduction of self-government, all magistrates (and mayors) of county (and city) governments have been elected directly by the people. Their tenure of office was originally set for three years. It has been extended to four years since the fourth election. The average turnout of voters in the past elections was about 74.74%. Responsibilities of a magistrate or a mayor include discharge of duties concerning local self-government, execution of commissions from governments at higher levels and direction and supervision of subordinate *hsiang, chen* and townships in matters concerning self-government.

The chiefs of *hsiang, chen* and townships have also been elected through popular vote. There is in each *hsiang, chen* or township a council consisting of representatives elected by the residents, which meets regularly to make reviews and interpellations of the activities of the *hsiang, chen* or township office.

LAND RESOURCES

AREA, GEOGRAPHICAL POSITION AND
TOPOGRAPHY

The Republic of China is situated in the east of Asia. It has a total area of 11,418,174.19 square kilometers.

Taiwan lies between 119° 18'03" and 122° 06'25" east longitude and 21° 45'25" and 25° 37'53" north latitude. It is bounded on the east by the Pacific Ocean. The Philippine Islands to the south of it is a nearby neighbor. To the west across the Taiwan Straits is Fukien Province. About 300 nautical miles northeast of it is the Ryukyu Islands.

The area of the island of Taiwan is 35,779 square kilometers. Plus the Penghu Islands, Lu Tao, Lan Hsu, Liuchiu Hsu and other offshore islands, the total size of the Taiwan Area comes up to 35,981 square kilometers (Not including the 173.1 Sq. k m. of Kinmen and Matsu). Surrounded by seas on all sides, the island of Taiwan has a total coast line of 1,566 kilometers.

Taiwan is 377 kilometers long and 142 kilometers broad in its widest section. The Central Range runs from the north to the south of the island, dividing it into two parts. Over two-thirds of the land area is over 100 meters above the sea-level.

The island is mountainous. There are 62 peaks with an elevation above 3,000 meters. Yu Shan, the highest of the mountains, rises 3,997 meters above the sea.

As is to be expected in view of the topography, the rivers on the island mostly have a steep incline over a rather short course. The longest river is the 170-kilometer Chuo Shui Chi. There are 20 other rivers with their length exceeding 50 kilometers.

LAND UTILIZATION

With the exception of the mountain lands, most of the island has been developed and utilized. In 1973, entries in the cadaster total 16,701 square kilometers, accounting for 46.42% of the island's total land area. Of this developed land, 87.90% or 14,682 square kilometers were used for crops, 6.14% or 1,025 square kilometers for construction, 3.19% or 532 square kilometers for communications and irrigation facilities; while the remaining 2.77% or 462 square kilometers were parks, levees and riverbeds. Thus, all level lands on Taiwan have in fact been put to full use. Hereafter, development of uplands and tidal lands will receive greater emphasis.

LAND REFORM

Farmland

Changes in the Incomes of Landlords and Tenants Since the Launching of the Land Reform Progran

Year	Yield	Division	of	the	Yield				
		Landlord				Tenant			
		Allotted share	Taxation in Kind	Net Gain	Index of Net Gain	Allotted share	Taxation in Kind	Land price paid in kind	Net Gain	Index of Net Gain
Before Rental Reduction 1948	3,894	Rental (3,894x50%)	229	1,718	100.0	1,947	—	—	1,947	100.0
After Rental Reduction 1949	4,248	Rental 1,947 (3,894x37.5%) 1,460	229	1,231	71.7	2,788	—	—	2,788	143.2
1950	4,822	1,460	229	1,231	71.7	3,362	—	—	3,362	172.7
1951	4,916	1,460	229	1,231	71.7	3,456	—	—	3,456	177.5
1952	5,216	1,460	229	LandPrice1,231 (3,894x30%)	71.7	3,756	—	—	3,756	192.9 2
After Launching of the Land-to-the-Tiller program 1953	5,388	—	—	△ 1,168	68.0	5,388	229	1,168	3,991	205.0
1954	5,562	—	—	△ 1,168	68.0	5,562	229	1,168	4,165	213.9
1955	5,472	—	—	△ 1,168	68.0	5,472	229	1,168	4,075	209.3
1956	5,786	—	—	△ 1,168	68.0	5,786	229	1,168	4,389	225.4
1957	5,968	—	—	△ 1,168	68.0	5,988	229	1,168	4,571	234.8
1958	6,174	—	—	△ 1,168	68.0	6,174	229	1,168	4,777	245.4
1959	6,062	—	—	△ 1,168	68.0	6,062	229	1,168	4,665	239.6
1960	6,366	—	—	△ 1,168	68.0	6,366	229	1,168	4,969	255.2
1961	6,604	—	—	△ 1,168	68.0	6,604	229	1,168	5,207	267.4
1962	6,851	—	—	△ 1,158	68.0	6,851	314	1,158	5,379	276.3
After Completion of 10-year Installment paymentory Land Price By the Tiller 1963	7,239	—	—		—	7,239	314	—	6,925	355.7
1964	7,537	—	—		—	7,537	314	—	7,223	371.0
1965	7,788	—	—		—	7,788	314	—	7,474	383.9
1966	7,673	—	—		—	7,673	314	—	7,359	378.0
1967	7,826	—	—		—	7,826	427	—	7,399	380.0
1968	8,142	—	—		—	8,142	437	—	7,705	395.7
1969	7,602	—	—		—	7,602	437	—	7,165	368.0
1970	8,128	—	—		—	8,128	437	—	7,691	395.0
1971	7,910	—	—		—	7,910	437	—	7,473	383.8
1972	8,364	—	—		—	8,364	432	—	7,932	407.4
1973	7,930	—	—		—	7,930	427	—	7,503	385.4

Source: Taiwan Provincial Food Bureau

Explanatory notes:

(1) The yields given in the table were those from one hectare of double-cropping paddy field.

(2) The net gains of the landlords after the lannching of the land-to-the-tiller program were the land price paid in kind by the tenants. These figures have been listed in the column to facilitate comparison.

(3) The price paid in kind by the tenants for land purchased compulsorily from landlords and resold to them was calculated at two and a half times the annual yield of the principal crop normally produced on the particular grade of land in each case (based on the standards adopted by county and city governments in implementation of rental reduction), plus an annual interest of 4%, to be paid by installments over a period of ten years.

(4) The base year for the index of net gain is 1948.

(5) Crop yield decreased in 1969 as a result of typhoon damage.

9

Rental Reduction

This program started in 1949. Its aim was to cut the exorbitant rentals, which ranged from 50% to 70% of the annual main crop yield, to a reasonable level. Under the program, farm rentals should not exceed 3.75% of the total annual yield of the main crop and that no deposit money and other extortionate charges should be collected from the tenant farmers. On this new basis, leases were signed for altogether 256,556 hectares of farmland, benefiting a total of 296,043 farm families.

Land-to-the-Tiller

(a) Sale of public land:

The program, started on a trial basis in 1948, was formally launched in 1951. The sales price of the public arable land was fixed at 2.5 times the annual main crop yield, to be paid in kind by installments over a period of ten years. Up to 1973, a total of 130,177 hectares had been sold to 276,781 farm families.

(b) Purchase and resale of private tenanted land:

In January 1953, the Province of Taiwan was formally designated by the Government as the area for starting the enforcement of the "Land-to-the-Tiller Statute." In accordance with the Statute, a landlord is allowed to keep no more than three hectares of medium-grade paddy field or six hectares of upland paddy field. Excess holdings are to be compulsorily purchased by the Government for resale to the incumbent tenant farmers at the same price as that of the public land. Consequently, 194,823 farm families purchased a total of 139,249 hectares of land and thus became the owners of the land they tilled.

(c) Results accomplished:

In 1953, per-hectare paddy rice yield was 5,388 kilograms. Exclusive of the 1,168 kilograms for installment payment of the purchased land, 4,220 kilograms were retained by the farmer, which was 2.2 times he kept for himself in 1948. In 1962, the land prices were fully paid up by the farmers, with the result that they began to have full title to the land they purchased. Thereafter, the entire crop yield of the land has belonged to the farmer. In 1973, the per-hectare yield was 7,930 kilograms, over four times that of 1948. (See accompanying table).

To safeguard the interests of the landlords, the purchase price of their land was paid up in rice and sweet potato bonds and shares of four large public industrial establishments, which were turned to private ownership as a consequence. Thus, large amounts of capital formerly tied up in land were channeled into industrial development. The boom in industry in recent years has further increased the gains of the former landlords.

Consolidation

In 1960-61, 4,179 hectares of farmland were consolidated under an experimental project. A ten-year program was launched in 1962 to consolidate 300,000 hectares. Up to the end of 1973, work on 259,324 hectares, about 85% of the total, was completed. (Land consolidation work was temporarily suspended in 1973.) Only 42% of the farm families on these farmlands had contiguous land holdings before the launching of the program. The percentage increased to 86% following the consolidation. Farmlands directly accessible by rural roads and irrigated increased from 20% to 100%, those with direct drainage, from 19% to 100%, the average size of the farm plots, from 0.07 hectares

to 0.25 hectare. The unit area yield of paddy rice gained by 32%, while a saving of 20% in labor was effected.

Urban Land

The purpose of urban land reform is to achieve equalization of land rights. First, the land values are to be announced publicly by the Government. Next, the owners are required to make their own assessment and declare their own prices to the Government. Then, if the owner of a piece of land has made too low an assessment, the Government will buy back his land at that value and make him suffer a loss; and, if he has made too high an assessment, the Government will collect taxes accordingly and make him lose through heavy taxes. According to the program, extra gains from the land shall revert to the community for use in promotion of public welfare.

Up to the end of 1973, a total of NT$8,766 million in land tax and NT$7,168 million in land value increment tax had been collected. With this money, social welfare funds have been instituted in various cities and counties, which are being used exclusively for financing public constructions and the nation's free education program.

HUMAN RESOURCES

GROWTH OF THE POPULATION

According to the household registration statistics, the population of Taiwan (not including aliens) was 15,564,830 (not including the 77,637 inhabitants of Kinmen and Matsu) at the end of 1973, as compared with 7,554,399 at the end of 1950. Of the 1973 population, 13,606,434 were living in Taiwan Province; 1,958,396, in Taipei City. Altogether 8,-175,327 or 52.52% were males; 7,389,503 or 47.48% were females. The population gained by 8,010,431 in a period of 23 years, the average annual increase being 340,000 persons.

The average annual rate of population increase was as high as 3.50% before 1959. It levelled off to 2.97% between 1960 and 1966, and has further lowered to 2.2% since 1967.

The birth rate in Taiwan has been dropping steadily over the years; so has also the mortality rate. The crude birth rate in 1950 was 43.29‰. It dropped to 23.79‰ in 1973. During the same period, mortality rate decreased from 11.47‰ to 4.76‰. The rate of natural population increase was 19.03‰ in 1973, showing a continual downtrend from 1971's 20.86‰ and 1972's 19.43‰. The statistics reflect that the promotion of family planning in Taiwan has already yielded gratifying results.

POPULATION DENSITY

In 1973, there were 432 persons to the square kilometer.

POPULATION DISTRIBUTION BY AGE AND EDUCATION

In 1973, working age (between 15 and 64) population number 9,292,216; young (14 and under) population, 5,769,199; and old (65 and over) population, 503,415. They respectively accounted for 59.70%, 37.07% and 3.23% of the total. The index of dependent population was 67.5, which means that there were 67.5 old or young people relying on 100 working age population for existence.

Of the 9,795,631 population aged 15 and over, 305,948 or 1.97% had received or were receiving university or higher education. Those graduated from or attending junior colleges, senior middle or senior vocational schools, junior middle and junior vocational schools numbered 336,429 (2.16% of the total), 1,519.044 (9.76%) and 1,352,704 (8.69%) respectively. The 4,197,158 graduates from primary schools made up the largest group, accounting for 26.97%; 388,450 (2.50%) had only little education, mostly through self-study; 1,695,898 (10.90%) were illiterates.

Employed persons increased by 260,000 annually in the past decade. As of the end of 1973, 37% of the employed were engaged in agriculture, 20% in industry, and 43% in communication, commerce and service.

NUMBER OF HOUSEHOLDS

At the end of 1973, there were altogether 2,865,801 households, of which 2,439,720 were in Taiwan Province and 426,081 in Taipei City. The average number of persons in each household was 5.43.

HUMAN RESOURCES

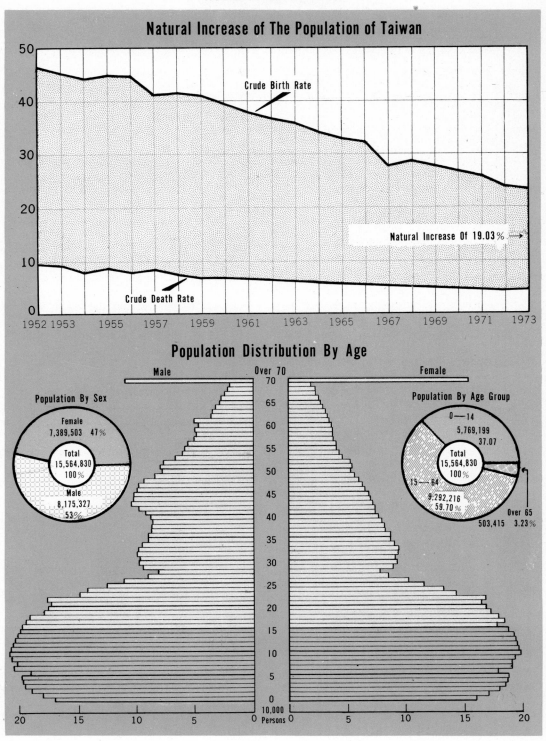

Natural Increase of The Population of Taiwan

Crude Birth Rate

Natural Increase Of 19.03% →

Crude Death Rate

1952 1953 1955 1957 1959 1961 1963 1965 1967 1969 1971 1973

Population Distribution By Age

Male   Over 70   Female

Population By Sex

Female
7,389,503 47%

Total
15,564,830
100%

Male
8,175,327
53%

Population By Age Group

0—14
5,769,199
37.07

Total
15,564,830
100%

15—64
9,292,216
59.70%

Over 65
503,415 3.23%

20   15   10   5   0   10,000   0   5   10   15   20

Persons

-13-

EDUCATION

HIGHER EDUCATION

Institutes of higher education include universities, colleges, junior colleges, and graduate schools. Their mission is to train specialists in various fields as required for socio-economic development and national reconstruction. There were only seven universities and colleges in academic year 1950 with a combined enrollment of 6,665 students. Since then educational expansion has been tremendous. As of academic year 1973 there were 99 institutes of higher learning providing education for 270,895 undergraduates and graduate students. The number of college graduates during academic years 1950-72 totalled 300,287.

SECONDARY EDUCATION

Secondary schools consist of junior and senior middle schools, normal schools and vocational schools:

Middle schools

There were 128 middle schools in academic year 1950 with a combined enrollment of 79,948 students, averaging 300 students per school. Both the number of schools and the size of enrollment grew steadily as the population kept expanding. In academic year 1973, there were 788 middle schools (including the public junior middle schools) with 1,140,260 students, averaging 1,447 students per school.

Normal schools

There were eight normal schools in academic year 1950. These schools were expanded and upgraded one by one to become junior teachers colleges for the sake of training more and better teachers for the primary schools. As of academic year 1973, there were nine junior teachers colleges with a total of 18,659 students (included in the higher education statistics) and one normal school with 1,241 students.

There were 77 vocational schools with 34,437 students in academic year 1950. By academic year 1973 the number of vocational schools had increased to 171 while total enrollment had risen to 232,574 students.

FREE EDUCATION

According to the Constitution, children shall attend schools for six years of free education upon reaching the age of six. There were 1,231 primary schools in academic year 1950 with a combined enrollment of 906,950 pupils, the attendance rate being only 79.98%. The past two decades witnessed

Number of Schools and Students(Academic year 1973)

Unit:Person

Location	Higher Education		Secondary Education		Primary Education		Pre-school Education	
	No. of Schools	Enrollment	No. of Schools	Enrollment	No. of Schools	Enrollment	No. of Schools	Enrollment
Grand total	99	270,895	959	1,374,075	2,349	2,431,440	618	110,977
Taipei City	21	93,348	98	213,977	107	274,000	117	33,052
Taiwan Province	78	177,547	850	1,152,572	2,200	2,140,852	498	77,266
Taipei County	13	43,328	72	99,881	145	221,356	62	13,333
Ilan County	1	1,620	30	37,399	29	68,427	15	2,181
Taoyuan County	6	12,197	52	69,855	128	130,643	24	3,308
Hsinchu County	6	9,712	47	37,219	105	93,982	28	5,150
Miaoli County	1	1,004	42	49,645	117	84,443	6	994
Taichung County	2	2,351	51	69,455	124	126,631	15	1,984
Changhwa County	3	1,737	54	82,242	159	167,998	14	2,830
Nantou County	1	400	39	42,314	144	82,572	15	1,793
Yunlin County	—	—	45	49,980	150	126,232	13	2,317
Chiayi County	4	6,877	58	72,530	151	134,651	37	4,928
Tainan County	7	11,239	64	79,318	125	143,688	62	4,409
Kaohsiung County	3	6,227	50	70,694	133	142,142	19	3,657
Pingtung County	5	7,505	55	74,529	161	139,062	35	4,558
Taitung County	1	1,207	28	22,952	110	49,923	17	1,361
Hualien County	1	1,722	31	31,109	118	54,582	10	1,608
Penghu County	—	—	15	9,585	43	19,692	11	1,352
Keelung City	3	7,092	18	33,981	36	53,236	13	3,403
Taichung City	13	40,695	30	54,890	40	77,500	28	5,168
Tainan City	2	9,445	32	54,046	33	77,222	31	6,884
Kaohsiung City	6	13,189	37	91,018	49	146,870	43	6,048
Fukien Province	—	—	11	7,526	42	16,588	3	659
Kinmen County	—	—	6	6,158	25	13,221	3	659
Lienkiang County	—	—	5	1,368	17	3,367	—	—

Note: The National Overseas Middle School is included in the statistics of Taiwan Province: the Affiliated Middle School of the National Taiwan Normal University is included in the statistics of Taipei City. The Affiliated Primary School and the Kindergarten of Taiwan Provincial Junior Teachers College are included in Taipei City's statistics because of their location.

a sharp rise both in the number of schools and attendance rate. As of academic year 1973 there were 2,349 primary schools with 2,431,440 pupils, the attendance rate being 98.09%.

To further upgrade the quality of the citizenry, the Government in academic year 1968 took an epochal step by adding another three years to the six-year free education in Taiwan Province, Taipei City, and the offshore islands of Kinmen and Matsu.

A school zone system was introduced under the nine-year free education program. Five hundred and seventy-six school zones were created between academic years 1968 and 1973 (522 zones in Taiwan Province, 46 in Taipei City, five on Kinmen, and four on Matsu) with one public junior middle school for each zone. In addition, there were ten private junior middle schools, with altogether, as shown in secondary education statistics, 18,080 classes and 948,872 students in academic year 1973.

PRE-SCHOOL EDUCATION

At the pre-school level, there were only 30 kindergartens with 17,111 children in academic year 1950. Along with economic prosperity has come increased attention to pre-school education. As a result, the number of kindergartens had increased to 618 by academic year 1973 with a combined enrollment of 110,977 children.

RATIO OF ADVANCEMENT TO THE NEXT HIGHER LEVEL OF SCHOOLING

In academic year 1973, 84.26% of primary school graduates went to junior middle schools, 65.43% of junior middle school graduates sought further education in senior middle schools and vocational schools, and 74.84% of senior middle school graduates were admitted to universities and colleges.

EDUCATIONAL INVESTMENT

Investment in educational, cultural, and scientific projects at the provincial level has been in excess of 35% of the government budget as stipulated in the Constitution. Substantial increase in educational outlays has been registered since the introduction of the nine-year free schooling program in academic year 1968. In academic year 1973 educational investment at various government levels consisted of NT$1,338,522,000 for the Central Government, NT$1,825,386,000 for the Taipei City Government, NT$ 2,368,622,000 for the Taiwan Provincial Government and NT$5,713,511,000 for the governments of all counties and cities of Taiwan Province.

EDUCATION

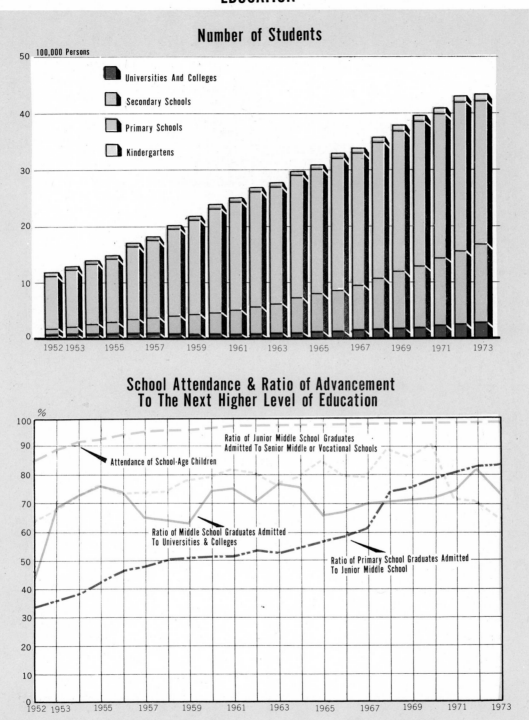

Number of Students

100,000 Persons

- Universities And Colleges
- Secondary Schools
- Primary Schools
- Kindergartens

School Attendance & Ratio of Advancement
To The Next Higher Level of Education

%

Ratio of Junior Middle School Graduates
Admitted To Senior Middle or Vocational Schools

Attendance of School-Age Children

Ratio of Middle School Graduates Admitted
To Universities & Colleges

Ratio of Primary School Graduates Admitted
To Junior Middle School

SCIENCE DEVELOPMENT

A National Council for Long-Range Science Development was set up by the Government in 1959 for advancement of science with a view to hastening the modernization of the nation. In 1967, a Committee for Science Development was activated by the National Security Council. Besides formulating the general policy for science development and mapping out a 12-year long-range program, the Committee had the National Council for Long-Range Science Development reorganized into the National Science Council for promotion of the following work:

Improve science education, and cultivate and recruit talent needed for carrying on science development activities in all sectors and at all levels;

Step up scientific research (or any other academic research) and foster high-caliber science research workers; and

Promote or support studies of applied science that have a bearing on the national economy.

Measures adopted included:

Advancement of science education and cultivation and recruitment of talent for taking up work in scientific fields:

Selection of on-the-job science researchers and teachers for advanced studies abroad: Up to the end of 1973, 898 persons had been sent abroad including 437 in natural science and engineering, 276 in medicine and agriculture, 171 in humanity and social science and 14 in science education.

Provision of research grants: Applications for support of research projects submitted by researchers in various universities and colleges and research institutes are accepted and screened by the National Science Council, with grants-in-aid made for the approved projects. Up to the end of 1973, researchers receiving the grants numbered 11,991, including 6,771 professors and 5,220 instructors and assistants.

Engaging of visiting professors: In academic year 1973, altogether 1,059 visiting professors and associate professors were engaged from abroad.

Translation of scientific works and other books for university and college students: Annual appropriations are made to the National Institute of Translation and Compilation for this purpose, with the translation of 115 works already completed.

Establishment of a Scientific Instrument & Data Center: The purposes of this Center are to provide assistance and support for science teaching and research, accommodate industries with scientific data and instruments, and promote the local manufacture of scientific instruments.

Promotion of science education in middle and primary schools:

(a) Upgrading the quality of science teachers: Training programs have been conducted for 50,420 primary school teachers and 1,830 middle school teachers. Under the joint sponsorship of the National Science Council and the Ministry of Education, 54 selected primary school science education personnel visited the United States or Japan on inspection tours, and the National Science Council has been granting financial support to middle school science and vocational training teachers for one-year advanced study in the United States and organized observations trips to the United States and Japan for selected middle school science education personnel.

(b) Improvement of teaching materials for middle and private schools: Projects for primary schools included the experimentation with science teaching materials at 27 selected schools to provide a basis for the revision work and study of such well-known educational research schemes as the AAAS schemes of the United States for reference purposes. Those for middle schools included the experimentation with new science teaching materials at 24 public junior middle schools and revision of the curricula for basic sciences at junior and senior middle schools.

Basic Science Research:

Promotion of basic theoretical studies: With the assistance and support of the National Science Council, five scientific research centers respectively for prosecution of theoretical studies in the fields of mathematics, physics, chemistry, biology and engineering were set up. Each composed of two or three well-established institutes of the universities. These centers have effectively avoided duplication of research efforts, and undertaken the all-important task of fostering research workers. Papers on studies already completed numbered over 500. Up to the academic year 1973, 1,268 researchers obtained their master degrees and 9 had doctorates conferred on them.

Moreover, geological surveys were carried on by the Institute of Geology of the National Taiwan University and the Department of Geological Science of the National Cheng Kung University, Taiwan

Provincial Institute of Geological Survey and the Chinese Petroleum Corporation. Meanwhile, geophysical studies were conducted separately by the Chinese Petroleum Corporation and the College of Science of the National Central University. And research in atmospheric science with special emphasis on typhoon problems was done simultaneously at the Institute of Physics of the Academia Sinica, the Department of Atmospheric Science of the National Taiwan University, College of Science of the National Central University, the Central Weather Bureau and the Meteorological Agency of the Chinese Air Force. More recently, with the support of the National Science Council an Institute of Biochemistry was jointly set up by the Academia Sinica and the National Taiwan University, with a view to laying a more adequate foundation for biological, agricultural and medical studies.

Grants for Financing Purchase of Research Equipment: This grants-in-aid program was instituted by the former National Council for Long-Range Scientific Development. Applications by public and private universities, colleges and research institutes are accepted, with grants made upon approval.

Research in Humanity and Social Science:

To meet the economic development needs, studies on specific projects in the fields of economics, political science, law, sociology, education and psychology have been actively promoted by the National Science Council. Subjects on which studies have already been completed or are being carried on number over 20 in all, including: an interdisciplinary study of national and cultural histories of Taiwan, a textual research on old Chinese books and records, the United States of America, the Dark Continent, Developments in Chinese Mainland under the Communist Regime, legal precedents, utilization of land resources in Taiwan, and Tiao-Yu-Tai Isles. In addition, the National Science Council has also extended substantial assistance to the Institutes of Economics of the Academia Sinica and the National Taiwan University.

Research in Applied Sciences and Development of Technology:

Research in these fields have been actively promoted by the National Science Council, Ministry of Economic Affairs, Ministry of Communications and Joint Commission on Rural Reconstruction, with emphasis laid on a number of specific projects as follows:

In the field of industry and mining: Main efforts have been directed at research in energy resources, minerals, iron and steel, metals and machinery, petrochemicals and high molecular weight chemicals, electricity, textiles and food processing. The work is being carried on by the Union Industrial Research Institute, Mining Research Institute and Metal Industrial Research Institute of the Ministry of Economic Affairs, the laboratories of various public and private industries and several independent research organizations.

In the field of agriculture: Work is carried on by the agricultural experimentation setups of relevant agencies of the Taiwan Provincial Government, with the Joint Commission on Rural Reconstruction as the coordinator. Among the more important research projects are culture of pest-and-disease-resistant, drought-resistant, chilling-resistant, early maturing varieties of major crops, cultivation and utilization of forestry resources, exploration of fishing resources and culture of marine products, hog breeding experiments, a study of animal diseases native to Taiwan, irrigation of sandy hills, water requirements for paddy rice irrigation and testing and extension of farming machines. In addition, grants were made to the Colleges of Agriculture of the National Taiwan University and the National Chung Hsing University for purchasing additional laboratory equipment, increasing library collections, and promoting basic agricultural research work. The Taiwan Sugar Corporation is, meanwhile, independently conducting hog-raising research and experiments on improvement of sugar cane varieties.

In the field of communications: Studies are being undertaken by the Taiwan Provincial Highway Bureau, Taiwan Railway Administration and Keelung and Kaohsiung Harbor Bureaus with respect to application of telecommunications science, highway construction planning, railroading, harbor engineering and meteorological problems. The Telecommunications Research Institute is well equipped; by order of the Ministry of Communications, 2% of the total revenue from the telecommunication services is appropriated annually to finance the Institute's research and development projects.

In the field of medical science and public health: Emphasis has been placed on drugs fighting cancerous growths, and diseases to which the Chinese race is particularly susceptible, reproduction and population problems, nutrition of the people, basic medical science (immunization and anatomy), and cure for bites from venomous snakes. The work is carried on by the National Defense Medical College and the College of Medicine of the National Taiwan University with the financial support of the National Science Council. Activities for promotion of public health consist mainly in environmental sanitation investigation and research to meet the actual needs of the different places. The agencies in charge are the experimentation organizations of the Taiwan Provincial Health Department and the Department of Public Health of the Taipei City Government.

Oceanography: With the support of the National Science Council, an Institute of Oceanography was set up by the National Taiwan University for conducting research in marine biology, marine geology and geophysical oceanography and physical oceanography. The National Science Council has further provided the Institute with a research vessel and also financial assistance for its operation.

Electronics: Emphasis is on the manufacture of newly developed integrated circuits and semiconductor materials, computers, electronic telecommunication switching system and computerization of material in the Chinese language.

Seismology: A ten-year plan for establishment of a telemetering seismic network was launched by the National Science Council, with a number of Chinese specialists engaged from the United States for its implementation. The construction of 17 seismic stations and three subcenters has been completed. Meanwhile, a project for research of earthquake engineering is being actively promoted.

Ship model testing: This is a fundamental work item in shipbuilding technology. With a grant from the National Science Council, the College of Engineering of the National Taiwan University has constructed a 150-meter-long ship model testing tank. In academic year 1973, a Shipbuilding Institute was inaugurated for fostering high-caliber shipbuilding engineers.

Sino-American Cooperation in Science and Technology:

To facilitate exchange of scholars and promote the intercourse between the academies and research institutes of the two countries, the Republic of China and the United States of America concluded in January 1969 an agreement for promotion of mutual cooperation in science and technology. The organizations responsible for the promotional work on the Chinese side is the National Science Council and that on the American side, National Science Foundation. To meet the actual needs in implementation of the program, a Special Assistant

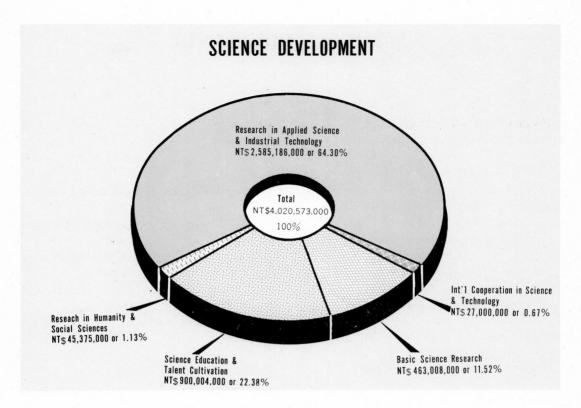

SCIENCE DEVELOPMENT

Research in Applied Science & Industrial Technology
NT$ 2,585,186,000 or 64.30%

Total
NT$ 4,020,573,000
100%

Int'l Cooperation in Science & Technology
NT$ 27,000,000 or 0.67%

Reseach in Humanity & Social Sciences
NT$ 45,375,000 or 1.13%

Science Education & Talent Cultivation
NT$ 900,004,000 or 22.38%

Basic Science Research
NT$ 463,008,000 or 11.52%

to the Ambassador for Science and Technology was assigned to the American Embassy in China by the U.S. State Department to render necessary consultant services. Meanwhile, a liaison officer bearing the official title of Counsellor of the Embassy for Science and Technology was dispatched to the United States by the National Science Council. Research projects conducted under the cooperative program include the artificial propagation of mullet fish, nutrition of women and children, ecological study for rice elongation (Bakanae) disease, research on uterus cancer and a study on plant life in Taiwan. Two symposiums under the program, one on ocean resources and the other on forest ecology and genetics, were held in Taiwan in 1971 and 1972 respectively, with a number of American experts participating. Another seminar was held by Chinese and American specialists in 1971 in the United States for discussion of typhoon problems. The subject matters of these symposiums were of mutual interest to the two countries and in the realm of applied science. Up to the end of 1973, American scientists and scholars visiting Taiwan under the cooperative program numbered 78, including three Nobel prize winners; Chinese scholars sent to the States on exchange-of-visits basis totalled 35.

SOCIAL INSURANCE

The government employees' insurance program was instituted in 1958, with a view to safeguarding the well-being of government employees and their dependents. The insured persons include all civil service functionaries and educational workers. (Military personnel have their own insurance system.) Benefits provided for include cash compensation and free medical care, the former being paid for disability, old-age and funeral allowance and the latter available on occasions of maternity, sickness and injury. The Government paid 65% of the premium on behalf of the insured.

At the end of 1959, 189,271 persons were insured under the program, including 35,377 Central Government employees and 153,894 local government employees; benefits paid out under the program totalled NT$56,260,000, including NT$46,929,000 for medical services and NT$9,331,000 in cash benefits. By the end of 1973, the number of insured persons increased by 77.29% to 335,558 persons, including 85,757 Central Government employees and 249,801 local government employees; benefits increased by 13.2 times to NT$796,584,000, including NT$336,615,000 for medical services and NT$459,969,000 in cash benefits.

LABOR INSURANCE:

In the interest of social stability, labor insurance was instituted by the Government in 1950. It was started in that year with a program for industrial workers; and later in 1951, 1953 and 1956, programs for professional (irregularly employed) workers, fishermen and sugarcane farmers were successively incepted. Since 1965, in accordance with the "Present-Stage Social Policy Formulated Along the Guidelines of the Principle of People's Livelihood," insurance has also been made available to government agencies and public schools. Since January 1970, employees of private firms, orchards, dairy farms, private schools, newspapers and other cultural media, cooperatives and private institutions have also been made eligible for protection by labor insurance.

An insured industrial worker has to pay only 20% of his premium, with the remaining 80% taken care of by the employers. For the irregularly employed professional workers, the Government pays 30% of the premium, with the remainder paid by themselves. For the fishermen's insurance program, the entire premium is paid out of the Fishermen's Insurance Reserve (funds made up with dues collected on fish catches put up for sale in the fish markets at 0.5-2.0% of the sales proceeds) in the case of fishermen engaged in deep-sea and inshore fisheries; half of the premium out of the reserve in the case of fishermen engaged in coastal and pond fisheries. Premiums for insurance of the sugarcane farmers are jointly paid by the employer and the farmer at the ratio

of 70% to 30%. Other insured workmen pay 20% of their premiums, with the Government taking care of the remainder.

The labor insurance programs provide benefits for childbirth, injury, sickness, disability, old age and death. The number of persons insured increased from 438,485 in 1957 to 1,380,885 in 1973. Included in the 1973 figure were 1,041,499 industrial workers, 64,347 professional workers, 141,609 fishermen, 53,526 office boys, technical workers and chauffeurs of government agencies and schools, 43,599 employees of private firms, orchards and dairy farms, 25,891 sugarcane farmers and 10,414 other kinds of workers. Benefits paid out increased from NT$54,060,000 in 1957 to NT$770,291,000 in 1973. For the latter figure, NT$83,160,000 were paid as maternity allowances: NT$23,898,000 for compensation to the injured, NT$62,719,000 for disability compensation, NT$197,355,000 as old-age retiring allowances, NT$218,938,000 for medical treatment of the sick, and NT$184,220,000 for death payments.

SOCIAL INSURANCE

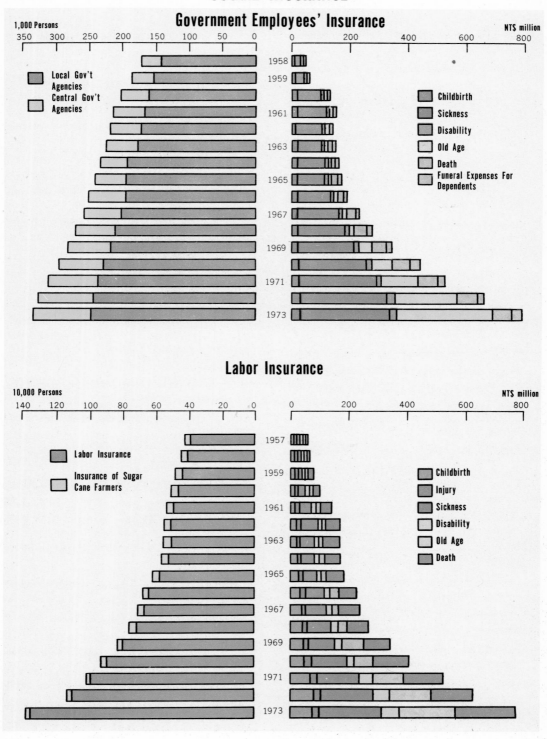

Government Employees' Insurance

1,000 Persons

350 300 250 200 150 100 50 0

NT$ million

0 200 400 600 800

Local Gov't Agencies
Central Gov't Agencies

Childbirth
Sickness
Disability
Old Age
Death
Funeral Expenses For Dependents

1958
1959
1961
1963
1965
1967
1969
1971
1973

Labor Insurance

10,000 Persons

140 120 100 80 60 40 20 0

NT$ million

0 200 400 600 800

Labor Insurance
Insurance of Sugar Cane Farmers

Childbirth
Injury
Sickness
Disability
Old Age
Death

1957
1959
1961
1963
1965
1967
1969
1971
1973

SOCIAL RELIEF

Social relief can be divided into emergency relief and charity programs. The former consists of emergency measures taken during a natural disaster (e.g., typhoon attack, earthquake and flood) to reduce losses of life and property and to rehabilitate the victims. The latter includes the providing of the helpless old people and children and crippled and disabled with food and accommodation in asylums and orphanages, and distribution of relief funds to needy families to meet their minimum living necessity. In its effort to step up social relief, the Government has taken steps to streamline the existent relief agencies on the one hand and actively encourage the participation of the private sector on the other. As a result, activities in this field are now making gratifying progress.

RELIEF AGENCIES:

By the end of 1973, there were altogether 90 in-

Inmates of Asylums of Relief Institutions

Year	Total		General Relief Institutions		Relief Institutions for Children		Veteran Homes	
	Number of Asylums	Number of Inmates	Number of Asylums	Number of Inmates	Number of Asylums	Number of Inmates	Number of Asylums	Number of Inmates
1953	28	8,440	17	3,608	7	1,003	4	3,829
1954	31	8,847	20	4,014	7	1,063	4	3,770
1955	33	9,112	21	4,091	8	1,232	4	3,789
1956	34	9,568	22	4,670	8	1,153	4	3,745
1957	36	11,233	22	4,938	8	1,476	6	4,819
1958	38	12,838	23	6,000	9	1,771	6	5,067
1959	45	15,139	25	6,387	12	2,128	8	6,624
1960	47	16,821	25	6,606	14	2,570	8	7,645
1961	50	18,243	27	6,828	15	2,742	8	8,673
1962	51	18,158	27	6,238	16	2,877	8	9,043
1963	53	19,301	27	6,617	17	3,020	9	9,664
1964	55	20,370	28	6,622	18	3,245	9	10,503
1965	59	21,962	30	7,030	20	3,544	9	11,388
1966	65	24,247	30	7,282	26	4,246	9	12,739
1967	70	25,925	28	7,203	33	5,306	9	13,416
1968	72	26,738	32	8,157	31	5,116	9	13,465
1969	75	27,529	30	8,158	35	5,594	10	13,777
1970	83	31,156	28	8,424	45	7,350	10	15,382
1971	91	35,400	28	9,061	53	7,116	10	19,223
1972	90	33,212	29	8,833	51	6,314	10	13,065
1973	90	31,047	30	6,416	49	6,346	11	18,285

stitutions engaged in relief work (30 public and private charity houses, 49 orphanages and 11 veteran homes) Inmates include (a) homeless old people and children, injured and disabled, impoverished and sick, people unable to earn a living and having no relatives to depend upon; (b) children that have suffered misfortunes; (c) aged and disabled ex-servicemen and veterans retired from active service because of old age or physical handicaps. At the end of 1973, inmates of these institutions totalled 31,047.

ASSISTANCE TO THE NEEDY:

This program is undertaken by various county

Assistance to the Needy

Year	Amount of Aid			Number of Aid Recipients		Percentage
	Total	In Cash (NT$ 10,000)	In Kind (NT$ 10,000)	Planned (10,000)	Actual (10,000)	
1956	269.8	172.6	97.2	74.3	64.9	87.4
1957	484.7	272.0	212.7	122.3	77.5	63.4
1958	643.0	367.7	275.3	116.0	82.4	71.0
1959	679.9	390.1	289.8	128.6	86.5	67.2
1960	828.7	436.8	391.8	137.1	92.5	67.5
1961	1,013.8	647.1	366.7	132.6	88.9	67.0
1962	1,093.6	681.1	412.5	134.9	87.0	64.5
1963	713.7	414.1	299.6	80.3	53.7	66.9
1964	1,168.2	726.8	441.4	89.5	71.9	80.4
1965	1,109.2	790.0	319.2	75.6	65.8	86.9
1966	1,302.2	863.8	438.4	67.2	59.7	86.7
1967	1,087.3	763.1	324.2	46.4	41.0	88.4
1968	1,642.9	1,233.8	409.1	50.1	47.9	95.5
1969	1,609.4	1,118.1	491.3	43.4	41.4	95.3
1970	1,806.0	1,318.1	487.9	39.0	38.4	98.6
1971	2,106.5	1,676.1	430.4	34.8	34.4	98.7
1972	2,329.9	1,977.8	352.1	32.9	31.7	96.3
1973	2,373.4	2,025.2	348.2	19.9	19.9	100.0

and city governments, with aid extended regularly to the following: (a) disabled and people unable to earn a living, (b) needy survivors of the military dead, and (c) needy families with more than five minor children. Aid includes supply of low-priced rice and grants of money, clothing and food.

AID TO VICTIMS OF CALAMITIES:

Aid is meted out to victims of such calamities as typhoons, floods, fires and earthquakes according to the need in the individual cases.

Aid To Victims of Calamites

Year	Number of Occurrences							No. of Victims	Casualities		Amount of Aid (NT$10,000)
	Total	Typhoon	Flood	Fire	Drought	Earth-quake	Ac-cident		Dead	Injured	
1957	49	4	1	32	—	10	2	1,934	34	51	7.7
1958	37	27	1	7	—	—	2	31,821	66	194	607.3
1959	113	9	7	82	—	7	8	393,242	784	566	3,611.5
1960	40	9	3	18	—	—	10	1,951	179	114	623.5
1961	32	9	1	15	—	1	6	19,498	276	436	1,220.1
1962	52	38	—	9	—	1	4	919	159	164	699.9
1963	52	3	—	46	—	2	1	1,471	230	107	628.4
1964	74	2	3	58	—	5	6	40,050	176	224	1,021.7
1965	73	4	—	64	—	1	4	28,058	117	296	856.6
1966	71	3	.3	64	—	1	—	1,633	114	63	323.6
1967	69	7	2	54	—	1	5	9,399	120	77	651.8
1968	73	8	7	54	—	—	4	3,045	101	40	499.2
1969	45	4	2	37	—	—	2	173,741	226	173	5,215.8
1970	24	1	—	23	—	—	—	4,822	112	34	522.6
1971	71	6	2	54	—	—	9	23,523	70	61	1,842.5
1972	45	10	4	31	—	—	—	21,344	87	14	623.8
1973	41	3	1	37	—	—	—	10,407	56	32	525.7

RELIEF FOR THE MAINLAND REFUGEES:

In response to President Chiang Kai-shek's call for extension of a helping hand to escapees from the mainland, the Free China Relief Association (FCRA), a private relief agency, was established in Taipei on April 4, 1950.

Thanks to the support of the Government and compatriots at home and abroad and th ssistance from international relief and philanthropic institutions, FCRA's activities have been steadily expanding over the past 20 years. Its achievements may be appraised roughly by a review of the number of its beneficiaries and the number of cases FCRA has rendered services:

Item	Accumulated No. of beneficiaries based on personal instances	Accumulated No. of cases based on service rendered
Inhabitants on Off-Shore Islands	485,553	2,246,537
Refugees in Hongkong & Macao	768,064	3,295,757
Refugees in Foreign Lands	506,613	869,806
Refugees Resettled in Taiwan	482,081	1,365,859
Victims of Calamities in Taiwan	239,954	633,079
Total	2,482,261	8,411,038

VOCATIONAL ASSISTANCE

For improving the overall vocational training system and the methods and techniques used in providing vocational assistance, the Government has adopted the following measures:

IMPROVEMENT OF VOCATIONAL TRAINING SYSTEM:

Promulgation of the Vocational Training Fund Statute, which provides that vocational training is obligatory on 91 categories of industry, and requires that every enterprise employing 40 or more persons should make regular contributions to the Fund equivalent to no less than 1.5% of its payroll;

Promulgation of the Vocational Training Law with a view to instituting uniform planning and promotion of vocational training so as to avoid duplication of efforts;

Encouragement of establishing training facilities by large enterprises and promotion of a network of industrial training facilities;

Assistance to small and medium-sized industries to help them join forces in conducting training activities;

Promotion of the expansion of the existing training centers and conducting of evening extension classes for factory workers of the various vocational and middle schools, adjustment of their curricula and length of training period, and streamlining of their procedures for admission of new students;

Assignment of new conscripts to various branches of the armed forces according to their training and strong points, and utilization of the facilities in the military establishments for training of the conscripts to better equip them for gainful employment after their release from the military service;

Promulgation of the Regulations Governing the Industrial Apprentice Training System;

Holding skill contests and encouraging participation in international skill contests, with a view to upgrading the level of skilled labor;

Establishment of a Modern Farming Training Center to step up training in mechanized farming to meet the manpower requirement under the Program for Rural and Agricultural Development.

IMPROVEMENT OF VOCATIONAL ASSIST-ANCE METHODS AND TECHNIQUES:

Improvement of the techniques for interviewing job-seekers so as to place the right men in the right jobs;

Introduction of a sound labor clearance system, and establishment of job banks so as to effectively regulate manpower supply and demand;

Rendering assistance to public middle schools for improvement of vocational guidance work, development of testing equipment and compilation of employment guidebooks;

Encouraging visits and establishing relationship with employers and providing them with related technical and consultation service;

Publication of job opportunities and job-seekers on a regular basis for the reference of both the job-seekers and the prospective employers;

Promotion of job analysis and formulation of job classification criteria in accordance with the national classification standard;

Promotion of the program for encouragement of the founding of new productive enterprises by young people, stepping up technical assistance and easing the terms of loans.

Agencies handling vocational assistance in the Central Government are the Ministry of Interior, Vocational Assistance Commission for Retired Servicemen (VACRS) and Vocational Assistance Commission for Youths (VACY); in the local governments, the relevant activities are under the charge of pertinent organizations of the Taiwan Provincial Government and Taipei City Government. The Ministry of Interior is responsible for formulation of the relevant laws and regulations and supervises the vocational assistance work carried on by the local governments. The VACRS renders vocational assistance to retired servicemen, provides educational and training opportunities for the veterans, and provides them with medical care and also sanitariums. The VACY deals mainly with vocational training and job placement for graduates of middle schools and higher educational institutions and matters of training and vocational guidance for high-caliber personnel, while the relevant local government agencies handle similar matters for the working age population in general.

Vocational Assistance for the General Public:

Specialized agencies set up by the Taiwan Provincial Government and Taipei City Government for providing vocational assistance to working-age population under their respective territorial jurisdiction comprise five vocational assistance centers and 12 employment service stations in Taiwan Province and one vocational assistance center and four employment service stations in Taipei City. Their functions include job placement, vocational training and vocational guidance. Up to the end of 1973, 1,205,906 job-seekers had registered with these agencies and vacancies advertised through them numbered 1,709,146. Persons placed by the agencies in the nine-year period totalled 593,466, or 66.06% of the registered job-seekers.

Vocational Assistance for the Retired Servicemen:

The VACRS's activities include the provision of employment service, medical care, vocational training and home for retired servicemen. Among its 97 subsidiaries are 41 productive enterprises, 13 medical units, eleven sanitariums, ten training institutions and 22 service centers. From 1952 to 1973, altogether 232,889 retired servicemen received VACRS's assistance, including 148,466 given employment, 64,507 provided with medical care, 17,119 settled in sanitariums, and 2,797 admitted to schools and training classes.

Vocational Assistance for Youths:

VACY aims primarily at recruitment of high-caliber talent from among the nation's citizens and Chinese nationals residing overseas, rendering of employment service to graduates of universities, colleges, and middle and vocational schools, and extension of assistance to promising young entrepreneurs. During the period from its activation in 1966 to the end of 1973, a total of 164,483 persons were placed in employment by VACY, including 1300 returned students, 296 local highly trained persons, 20,835 college and university graduates, 9,005 senior middle (or vocational) school graduates, 122,942 public junior middle school graduates and 10,105 graduates from other junior middle (or vocational) schools.

HEALTH CARE & ENVIRONMENTAL SANITATION

MEDICAL SERVICE AND REGISTERED MED-
ICAL PERSONNEL:

In 1952, Taiwan had altogether 578 public hospitals and clinics (statistics on privately owned and operated hospitals and clinics are unavailable). By the end of December 1973, there were 640 public and 10,859 private hospitals and clinics, adding up to 11,499, equipped with a total of 25,098 bed.

Registered physicians totalled 5,049 in 1952, averaging one for every 1,608 population. By the end of 1973, the total number increased by 7,746 to 12,795, averaging one for every 1,216 population according to the census taken at that time.

Year	Total	Physicians	Herb Doctors	Dental Surgeons	Pharma-ceutists	Nurses	Midwives	Junior Druggists	Dentists
1952	11,076	5,049	1,655	722	865	741	2,044	—	—
1973	44,274	12,795	3,095	2,026	4,850	11,537	8,676	1,025	290

CONTROL OF COMMUNICABLE DISEASE:

Malaria Prevention:

On average there were 1,200,000 malaria cases every year during the period 1947-1952. After the enforcement of a malaria prevention campaign featured by house-to-house spraying of DDT to extinguish malaria-carrying mosquitoes and free medical treatment to the infected during a four-year period beginning in 1952, the result was most gratifying as the Taiwan Area has since been free of malaria. In 1965, Taiwan was certified by the World Health Organization (WHO) as an area where malaria had been successfully eradicated.

Trachoma Control:

A program for prevention of the spread of trachoma among middle and primary school students was launched in 1954 with the assistance of the United Nations Children Welfare Fund (UNICEF) and WHO with free treatment given to the infected. By the end of 1973, trachoma incidence dropped from the original 73.5% to 4.46%. The preventive work has now been extended to the general public.

T. B. Control:

In 1947, tuberculosis was the cause of 285.2 deaths among every 100,000 population. Since then, steady efforts have been made to step up the preventive work, with a special agency set up for its promotion, roving X-ray and BCG inoculation teams organized to extend the work to governmental offices, schools and other organizations, and the masses adequately educated in public and personal hygienes. As a result, the deaths caused by tuberculosis among 100,000 population reduced to 46.3 by 1959 and further to 25.5 in 1973.

PREVENTIVE VACCINATION:

In addition to stepping up the improvement of environmental sanitation, preventive inoculation and vaccination has been greatly strengthened so as to stamp out communicable diseases. The number of persons receiving inoculation and vaccination increased from 2,932,010 in 1953 to 14,600,080 in 1973.

LEGAL COMMUNICABLE DISEASES AND THEIR MORTALITY RATES:

With the effective preventive work done over the years and persons receiving vaccination steadily increasing, the incidence of the communicable diseases and their mortality rates have been dropping sharply since 1957. In 1956, 1,547 persons were infected, of whom 237 died. By 1973, the incidence was lowered to 198, of whom only nine died. Covered by the 1973 statistical data were 75 infected with typhoid and paratyphoid, 93 with diphtheria, (of whom four died), 27 with dysentery (of whom two died), three with encephalitis (which proved fatal to all three). No cases of other legal communicable diseases were reported during the year.

ENVIRONMENTAL PROTECTION:

Environmental protection means the prevention of such public nuisances as air and water pollution, contamination of the soil, disturbing noices, offensive odors that affect the people's living conditions and health.

Successful implementation of the economic development plans on Taiwan has led to a continued boom in industry, rapid urbanization and a steady increase in motor traffic, with the consequence that air and water, as well as earth, have all become contaminated to a certain degree. To protect the people from these potential hazards, environmental

control has thus been exercised by the National Health Administration. Steps taken include:

Drafting of the following environmental control laws and regulations:

(a) Statute for Air Pollution Control,

(b) Environmental Protection Law,

(c) Regulations Governing Waste Disposal,

(d) Statute for Water Pollution Control, and

(e) Regulations Governing the Installation of Sanitary Sewerage.

In addition, the Draft of a Noise Nuisance Law is now in preparation.

Abatement of Air Pollution:

Altogether 89 air pollution checking stations have been set up, of which 15 are located in Taipei City and 74 in Taiwan Province. Samples of air are regularly taken for various specific tests, with serious air contamination effectively prevented.

Prevention of Water Pollution:

The health authorities of the Taiwan Provincial Government and the Taipei City Government have been in charge of preventing contamination of rivers that supply drinking water as one of their priority assignments. Cases of factories discharging waste materials into rivers and those raising ducks and dumping rubbish along the river banks were effectively banned by the police. Meanwhile, inspection squads have been organized to make regular on-the-spot checks and give admonition against abuse of the environment.

AGGREGATE SUPPLY, AGGREGATE DEMAND AND ECONOMIC GROWTH

AGGREGATE SUPPLY AND DEMAND IN 1973:

In 1973, the aggregate supply and demand amounted to NT$511,293,000,000, up 26.61% from 1972. The aggregate supply was made up by gross domestic product (GDP) in the amount of NT$357,380,000,000 and imports of goods and services valued at NT$-153,913,000,000. The aggregate demand consisted of national consumption including government and private consumption in the amount of NT$236,921,-000,000, gross domestic capital formation amounting to NT$89,776,000,000 and exports of goods and services valued at NT$184,396,000,000.

AGGREGATE SUPPLY AND DEMAND DURING THE PAST FIVE FOUR-YEAR PLAN PERIODS:

The share of GDP in the aggregate supply decreased steadily over the years—being 87.56% under the First Four-Year Economic Development Plan (1953-56), 84.49% under the Second Plan (1957-60), 84.05% under the Third Plan (1961-64), 80.99% under the Fourth Plan (1965-68), 75.40% under the Fifth Plan (1969-72) and 69.90% during the first year (1973) under the Sixth Plan. The share of imported goods and services, on the conrary, increased steadily—being 12.44% under the First Plan, 15.51% under the Second Plan, 15.95% under the Third Plan, 19.01% under the Fourth Plan, 24.60% under the Fifth Plan and 30.10% during the first year under the Sixth Plan.

Aggregate Supply

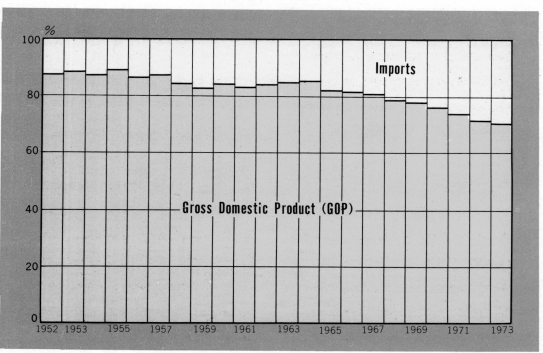

36

Composition of the aggregate demand under the past five four-year plans is as follows:

Period	National Consumption(%)	Capital Formation(%)	Exports(%)
1st Plan	79.98	12.97	7.05
2nd Plan	75.30	15.27	9.43
3rd Plan	70.96	15.92	13.12
4th Plan	63.09	19.63	17.28
5th Plan	54.60	19.29	26.11

These statistics show that the share of national consumption in the aggregate demand decreased steadily, whereas that of capital formation continued to gain and that of exports grew very rapidly. During the first year under the Sixth Plan, national consumption further lowered to 46.34% and capital formation also dropped slightly to 17.60% as a result of a decrease in inventory, while exports rose more quickly than ever to 36.06%.

CHANGES OVER THE YEARS

Little change occurred in the structure of the aggregate supply between 1951 and 1957, with GDP accounting for 86-88% and exports, 12-14% on the yearly average. However, since 1958, the share of imports has increased steadily, whereas that of GDP has been gradually on the decrease. At 1966 constant prices, goods and services imported in 1973 amounted to NT$111,397,000,000, 16.7 times larger than 1951's NT$6,281,000,000. On the other hand, GDP in 1973 (NT$255,771,000,000) was only 5.8 times larger than that in 1951 (NT$37,530,000,000).

Changes in the structure of aggregate demand have been much more significant. The share of national consumption in the aggregate demand ranged between 79% and 81% during 1951-55. However, it has been shrinking rapidly over the years since 1956. It was lowered to 72.56% in 1961, 64.34% in 1966, 49.62% in 1972 and further to 46.34% in 1973.

The share of capital formation ranged between 11% and 13% during 1951-57. It began to increase steadily in 1958, rising to 16.64% in 1961, 19.07% in 1966, 19.46% in 1971, but dropped slightly to 17.87% and 17.60% in 1972 and 1973 respectively. The share of exports showed different trends in three distinct phases: during the first phase which extended from 1951 to 1954, it gradually decreased from 8.86% to 5.63%; during the second phase which covered the years 1955 through 1961, it gradually increased from 7.29% to 10.74%; during the third phase which began in 1962, it rose rapidly from 10.94% to 32.51% in 1972 and further to 36.06% in 1973. At 1966 constant prices, the national consumption in 1973 was NT$162,981,000,000, up by 3.6 times from 1951's NT$35,363,000,000. Gross capital formation in 1973 was valued at NT$70,100,000,000, up by 14.1 times from 1951's NT$4,656,000,000. Exports in 1973 came to NT$134,081,000,000, up by 33.2 times from 1951's NT$3,923,000,000. Thus during the past 22 years, exports made the fastest advance, followed by capital formation. The share of national consumption has been declining significantly. These favorable developments have made possible the accelerated growth of the economy.

ECONOMIC GROWTH:

In terms of real gross national product (GNP), the rate of economic growth was 12.2% in 1952 and 10.32% in 1973. The average annual growth during the 22-year period was 9.13%.

Tabulated below are the economic growth rates for the years 1952 through 1973:

Economic Growth

Year	1952	1953	1954	1955	1956	1957	1958	1959	1960	1961	1962
Growth rate (%)	12.15	9.06	8.25	8.24	4.65	7.21	6.72	7.32	6.20	7.22	7.29
Year	1963	1964	1965	1966	1967	1968	1969	1970	1971	1972	1973
Growth rate (%)	9.55	12.13	11.60	8.55	10.33	9.28	8.73	11.17	11.40	11.45	12.32

Aggregate Demand

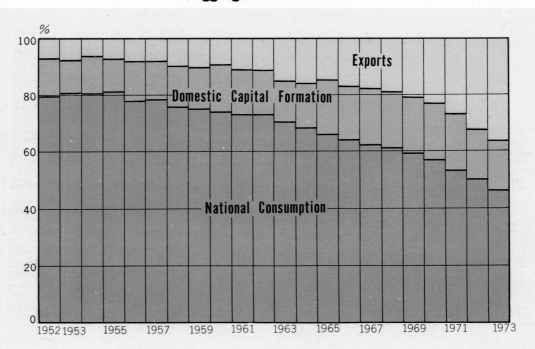

NATIONAL INCOME

National income of the Republic of China in 1973 was estimated to be NT$276,901,000,000 at current prices, showing a growth of 21.23% during the year. The rate of real growth in national income (at 1966 prices and after adjustment for gain or loss due to changed terms of trade) was 10.41%, higher than that of 9.66% in 1972.

The real income after adjustment for gain or loss due to changed terms of trade amounted to NT$-195,744,000,000 (at 1966 prices) in 1973, an increase of 4.94 times over 1951's NT$32,980,000,000. The average annual rate of growth in the real income was 8.47%. The highest annual growth rate, 15.49%, was registered in 1964, while the lowest annual growth rate was 4.65% of 1956.

The average growth rates of real national income after adjustment for gain or loss due to changed terms of trade under the various four-year plans are as follows: 6.38% under the First Plan, 6.35% under the Second Plan, 10.62% under the Third Plan, 8.17% under the Fourth Plan, and 9.99% under the Fifth Plan.

Per capita income in 1973 was NT$17,855, an increase of 19.03% over NT$15,001 of 1972. In real terms (at 1966 prices and after adjustment for gain or loss due to changed terms of trade), the increase was 8.40%, larger than the 7.46% of 1972.

Net real per capita product increased by 2.21 times from 1951 to 1973, its average annual rate of growth during this 23-year period being 5.48%. The highest annual rate of growth was 10.82% in 1964, followed by 9.97% in 1973, 9.55% in 1971 and 8.41% in 1970. The lowest was less than 1% in 1956. During the same period, the real per capita income rose by 2.16 times, growing at an average annual rate of 5.41%. The highest annual rate of growth was 12.19% in 1964, followed by 10.10% in 1963. The lowest was somewhere about 1% in 1954, 1956 and 1958.

The average growth rate of net real per capita product under the First Four-Year Economic Development Plan was 2.84%. It rose to 3.47% under the Second Plan and again to 6.05% under the Third Plan, and went down slightly to 5.83% under the Fourth Plan. Under the Fifth Plan, the average advanced to 7.70%, the highest ever achieved during a four-year period. After adjustment for gain or loss due to changed terms of trade, the average growth rate of real per capita income was the highest under the Fifth Plan, being 7.60%, followed by 7.37% 5.17%, 3.03% and 2.72% of the Third, Fourth, Second and First Plans.

NATIONAL & PER CAPITA INCOME

National Income

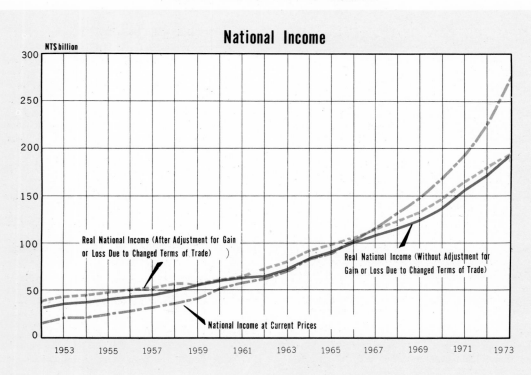

NT$ billion

Real National Income (After Adjustment for Gain or Loss Due to Changed Terms of Trade)

Real National Income (Without Adjustment for Gain or Loss Due to Changed Terms of Trade)

National Income at Current Prices

Per Capita Income

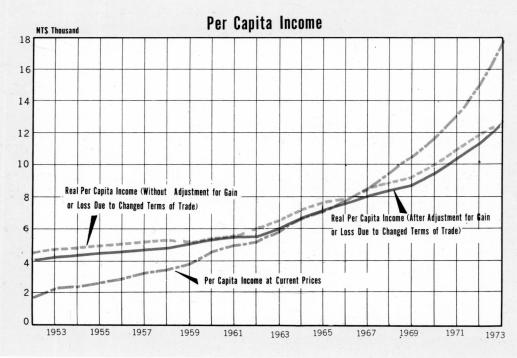

NT$ Thousand

Real Per Capita Income (Without Adjustment for Gain or Loss Due to Changed Terms of Trade)

Real Per Capita Income (After Adjustment for Gain or Loss Due to Changed Terms of Trade)

Per Capita Income at Current Prices

40

IMPLEMENTATION OF ECONOMIC DEVELOPMENT PLANS

To make effective use of available resources in order to accelerate economic growth, the Government started in 1953 a series of Four-Year Economic Development Plans. Up to the end of 1972, five consecutive four-year plans were successfully implemented. The following table shows the accomplishments under each plan by comparing the growth rates of the ending year of each with those of the year immediately before that plan was launched.

Accomplishments under the Five Past 4-Year Economic Development Plans

Item	1st 4-Year Plan (1953-56)	2nd 4-Year Plan (1957-60)	3rd 4-Year Plan (1961-64)	4th 4-Year Plan (1965-68)	5th 4-Year Plan (1969-72)
National Income	28.0%	27.9%	49.4%	35.7%	46.0%
Per Capita Income	11.3	12.6	32.6	22.3	33.8
Employment	2.7	10.9	10.9	16.9	15.1
Production					
Agriculture	21.4	18.0	24.3	27.0	8.5
Industry	55.4	57.4	67.5	96.0	111.7
Overland Transportation					
Freight	48.0	22.4	20.8	28.2	21.8
Passenger	75.6	31.5	23.1	41.3	34.5
Foreign Trade					
Imports	17.3	37.1	52.5	121.1	124.1
Exports	21.1	66.4	100.1	125.4	171.3

For the First Plan, investment actually made in agriculture, industry and transportation and communications was 98% of the planned investment. It was 101% for the Second Plan, 93% for the Third Plan, 124% for the Fourth Plan, and 137% for the Fifth Plan.

The current or Sixth Four-Year Plan extends from 1973 to 1976. In the Long-Range Economic

Devolopment Program for the Taiwan Area of the Republic of China, three principal guidelines are set forth for directing future efforts of the nation. They are: (1) to hasten the modernization of the economy, (2) to sustain growth and stability, and (3) to improve the living standard of the people. There has also been mapped out in the program a set of main targets as well as a number of supporting policy measures. Accordingly, the targets under the Sixth Plan were formulated largely on the basis of the projections in the long-range plan, with necessary adjustments made in the light of the current economic situation and the economy's future needs and potentialities.

Annual Growth Targets under the Sixth Four-Year Economic Development Plan

Item	Gross National Product	National Income	Per Capita Income	Population	Employment	Investment	Consumption	Imports	Exports
%	9.5	9.3	7.2	2.0	3.2	14.8	8.5	15.0	12.9

In order to achieve the above targets, the following basic policies and measures havev been adopted:

Modernization of Agriculture:

Improvement of the agricultural structure and enlargement of the operational scale;

Enhancement of agricultural productivity and increase of farm income;

Improvement of marketing system and regulation of the prices of agricultural products;

Improvement of farm credit system and increase in agricultural investment;

Reduction of the costs of farm requisites;

Improvement of the farmers' organizations to better serve the farmers;

Improvement of farmers' living conditions and promotion of farmers' welfare;

Strengthening of the setup for agricultural administration and cultivating of agricultural personnel.

Acceleration of Industrialzation:

Acceleration of the development of capital-intensive and high-technology industries;

Continued promotion of export industries and enhancement of their competitiveness in the world market;

Further improvement of the investment climate;

Promotion of rationalization of industrial enterprises;

Stepping up of industrial and applied science research.

Increased Emphasis on Transportation and Communications Development:

Implementation of the railway electrification project and increase of the railway's transportation capacity;

Continuation of the construction of the North-South Freeway and improvement of the road conditions of the existing trunk highway;

Expansion of the harbor facilities at Keelung and Kaohsiung and launching of the Taichung Harbor construction project;

Procurement of new vessels and improvement of the merchant fleet;

Expansion of existing airport facilities and construction of Taoyuan Airport;

Further improvement of the telecommunications services;

Improvement of the meteological facilities and strengthening of the weather forecasting service.

Effective Application of Fiscal Policy:

Adequate adjustment of public expenditures;

Improvement of the revenue sharing system between the various levels of government;

Adoption of performance budget and modernization of the treasury system;

Furtherance of the tax reform program.

Effective Use of Monetary Policy:

Increase of the responsibility and improvement of the functioning of the Central Bank in controlling money supply;

Attainment of a sound interest rate structure;

Modernization of banking services;

Encouragement of private savings;

Improvement of the short-term money market.

Strengthening of External Economic Relations:

All out trade promotion;

Liberalization of import control;

Effective management of foreign exchange;

Encouragement of medium and long-term capital inflow;

Encouragement of technical cooperation;

Strengthening of international economic cooperation.

Development of Human Resources:

Continued implementation of the Government's population policy;

Providing of more non-agricultural job opportunities for new labor market entrants and workers released from the farms by farm mechanization;

Strengthening of manpower cultivation and training;

Establishing of a national vocational training system and expanding of the scope of vocational training;

Effective enforcement of the social security system and expanding of the scope of employment service.

Implementation of Urban Development Plan:

Implemention of the regional development plan so as to achieve a balanced development among the various regions;

Establishment of the city-and-township system in the interest of a rational distribution of urban population.

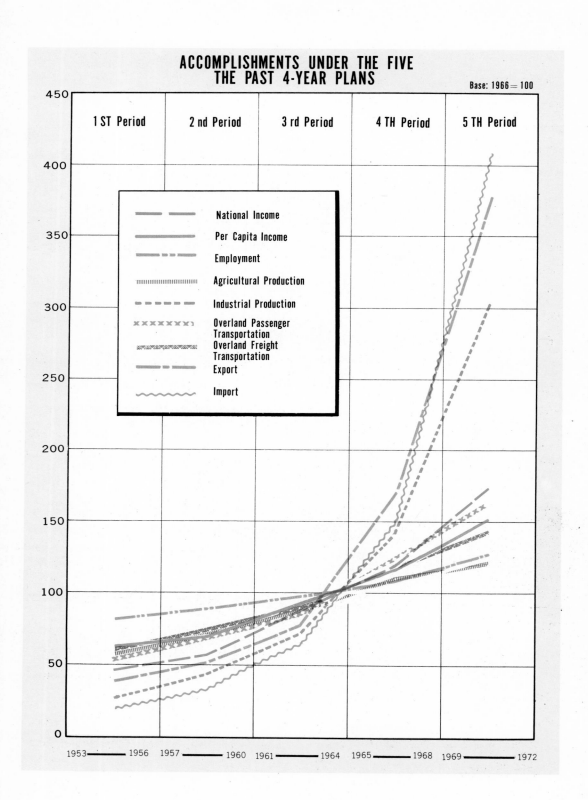

ACCOMPLISHMENTS UNDER THE FIVE
THE PAST 4-YEAR PLANS

Base: 1966 = 100

1 ST Period	2 nd Period	3 rd Period	4 TH Period	5 TH Period

National Income

Per Capita Income

Employment

Agricultural Production

Industrial Production

Overland Passenger Transportation

Overland Freight Transportation

Export

Import

1953 — 1956   1957 — 1960   1961 — 1964   1965 — 1968   1969 — 1972

44

ENCOURGEMENT OF INVESTMENT

For the acceleration of economic development, private industrial investment has been effectively encouraged, with three investment laws, namely, the "Statute for Encouragement of Investment," the "Statute for Investment by Overseas Chinese" and the "Statute for Investment by Foreign Nationals" enacted and subsequently amended according to the changed situation and needs. The main points of the laws are as follows:

THE STATUTE FOR ENCOURAGEMENT OF INVESTMENT:

A five-year income tax holiday for newly established productive enterprises which meet the encouragement criteria (and a 10% income tax deduction from the sixth year of its operation), or, as an alternative, an acceleration of the depreciation of fixed assets–both applicable also to cases of capacity expansion;

The maximum income tax payable by a productive enterprise to be limited to 35% of its total annual income;

Exemption from business tax for export sales;

Exemption from income tax for capital gains realized from sale of debentures held for more than two years;

Exemption from income tax for interest income accruing from savings deposit with a maturity of over two years;

Facilication of acquisition of land as plant sites.

STATUTE FOR INVESTMENT BY OVERSEAS CHINESES AND FOREIGN NATIONALS:

Repatriation of invested capital at the rate of 15% a year;

Approval of foreign exchange application for the entire returns from the investment;

Immunity from expropriation for ventures owned by overseas Chinese or foreign investors;

Enjoyment of treatment accorded to similar enterprises established by Chinese nationals;

No restrictions on the nationality and domicile of the managing directors;

Repatriation of capital in case the relevant investment project fails to materialize.

Other measures taken to improve the investment climate include simplification of the procedures and shortening of the time required for application for permission to effect an investment project, and facilitating of entry and exit by businessmen. Excellent social order and internal security are additional safeguards for investors' interests.

APPROVALS OF OVERSEAS CHINESE AND FOREIGN INVESTMENTS:

Good investment climate, rapid economic growth, continued improvement in the people's living standards and sound finances of the country have combined to induce a steady capital inflow. Back in 1952, investments by overseas Chinese amounted to a mere US$1,067,000 and there was no investment by foreigners. In 1973, overseas Chinese and foreign investments approved by the Government amounted respectively to US$55,166,000 and US$193,688,000. Over the years, approved overseas Chinese investments added up to US$282,456,000 and foreign investments, US$815,240,000, totalling US$1,097,696,000.

OVERSEAS CHINESE & FOREIGN INVESTMENT

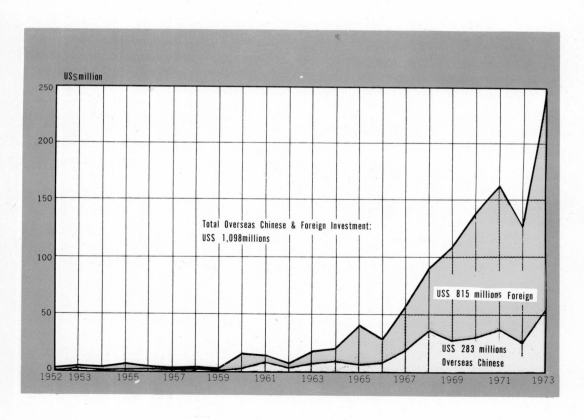

46

RURAL RECONSTRUCTION

The Joint Commission on Rural Reconstruction (JCRR) was set up jointly by the Government of the Republic of China and the United States in October 1946 in an effort to rehabilitate the rural economy in China after World War II. Financed by U.S. aid program in China prior to its termination in 1965 and thereafter by special appropriations from Sino-American Fund for Economic and Social Development (SAFED), JCRR started its operations on the mainland and has contributed significantly to rural reconstruction in Taiwan since its transference to this island in 1949.

Over the past years, JCRR has sponsored a total of 9,100 projects for development of agricultural resources, increase of agricultural production and improvement of the life of the farmers on Taiwan. As a result, the output of almost all farm products has been increasing steadily, with unit area yields of such important crops as rice, sweet potatoes, soybeans, pineapple and tea showing an average annual rate of growth of 2.2-5.2% since 1953 and the number of persons supported by each hectare of cultivated land rising from 9.3 to 17 during the same period.

To meet the long-range needs of the economy, JCRR has in recent years placed special emphasis on the following objectives:

a. Increase of food production to meet the increasing

Subsidies Provided in Various Years

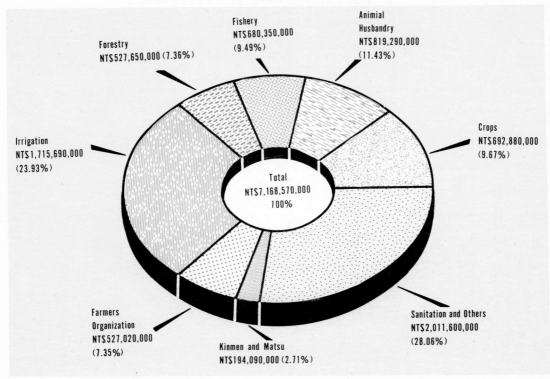

Forestry NT$527,650,000 (7.36%)

Fishery NT$680,350,000 (9.49%)

Animial Husbandry NT$819,290,000 (11.43%)

Irrigation NT$1,715,690,000 (23.93%)

Crops NT$692,880,000 (9.67%)

Total NT$7,168,570,000 100%

Farmers Organization NT$527,020,000 (7.35%)

Kinmen and Matsu NT$194,090,000 (2.71%)

Sanitation and Others NT$2,011,600,000 (28.06%)

requirement of the expanding population as well as to improve their nutrition;

b. Furtherance of agricultural exports and develop-ment of new export-oriented agricultural products;

c. Development of agricultural processing industry, so as to increase the employment of rural manpower and improve the life of the farming populace.

JCCR's promotional efforts, which take the form of research, direct sponsorship and provision of technical and financial assistance, have been actively supported by the Ministry of Economic Affairs and the Taiwan Provincial Department of Agriculture and Forestry. As a result, rural reconstruction work has been making good progress over the years. As a matter of policy, JCRR turns over each successful project to agencies concerned for further promotion, while always looking out for opportunities to start up new fruitful projects.

To accelerate agricultural development and to raise the living standard of the rural population, Premier Chiang Ching-kuo announced on September 27, 1972 a new rural reconstruction program. Collaboration among various government depart-ments along the lines of efforts conceived of by the Premier has made possible the attainment of the following gratifying results during the first year of the implementation of the program.

PROGRESS ACHIEVED IN THE FIRST YEAR OF IMPLEMENTATION OF THE PROGRAM FOR ACCELERATING RURAL AND AGRICULTURAL DEVELOPMENT

The specific measures were instituted under the program for accelerating rural and agricultural development. Three of these, namely, abolition of the rice-fertilizer barter system, abolition of the and surtax levied for educational purposes and relaxation of the terms of agricultural loans, involve institutional changes. By virtue of these measures, farmers are now having easier access to fertilizer and working capital so as to step up production. Insofar as the farmers' production cost is concerned, it is estimated that a saving of no less than NT$130 million a year by the farmers has been made possible by these measures - NT$100 million saved on interest by borrowing from the low-interest NT$1,830 million farm credit program and an NT$30 million expense spared as a result of the remission of the educational surtax.

The other six measures are: improvement of agricultural marketing, strengthening of rural infrastructure, acceleration of the extension of integrated use of improved cultural techniques, establishment of specialized agricultultural productioi areas, encouragment of the establishment of factories in rural areas, and strengthening of agricultural research and extension. A total of 188 projects have been approved for implementation of these six measures. Of the total, 62 have already been completed and 11 are near completion. However, most of the projects are continuous in nature. Completion of a project often means the pushing of a scheme forward from one stage to another. Thus, the following recounts of the progress achieved are based merely on a preliminary evaluation made of the benefits of the projects.

Improvement of Agricultural Marketing

The practice of joint marketing of agricultural products has enabled the farmers to command better salesprices. For example, in the twelve months of 1973, hogs sold through joint marketing totalled 204,000 head, which brought the farmers in an additional NT$44 million. For another example, packaging of vegetables by grades has been primarily introduced for adoption in specialized agricultural production areas, and the practice is likely to win general acceptance in the future.

To facilitate wholesale operations, two new wholesale markets, Hwa Kiang and Yang Ming, and a Provincial Farmers Association's farm produce handling yard were opened up in mid-1973.

Strengthening of Rural Infrastructure

Irrigation faecilities and fishing harbors:

The 22 projects programmed for the first stage of the program have all been completed. Six of these projects were for construction of sea dikes, including those in Changhua and Yunlin Counties and 19 kilometers elsewhere on the island, which are giving protection to 88,000 population, 13,000 houses, 8,400 hectares of farmland, over 1,000 hectare of fish ponds and more than 100 kilometers of highways and irrigation ditches.

Under three other flood control projects, some 9,400 meters of levees, 1,000 meters of retaining walls and 22 spur dikes were completed, safeguarding 4,000 hectares of farmland, 230 hectares of forests, 2,000 houses and 32,000 population, as well as two kilometers of railway tracks, 21 kilometers of highways, 70 kilometers of irrigation ditches and a number of schools, bridges and other structures in the neighborhoods.

The first stage of the Wangkung fishing harbor reconstruction project was completed and the Tahsi fishing harbor was in good repair. These facilitate berthing and add to the safety of fishing fleets in the nearby waters.

Construction of More Windbreaks:

At Meiliao Village of Yunlin County, where sandstorms frequently play havocs, long stretches of sand-arresting fence have been constructed on 116 hectares of beaches. As a result, there has been a marked lessening of sand-fall in the nearby inland areas.

In Taichung and Changhua Counties, lines of

trees totalling 1,253 kilometers in length have been planted as windbreaks, giving protection to 24,000 hectares of farmland. It is estimated that this will mean NT$56 million additional income to 32,000 farmer-beneficiaries.

Development of Slope Lands and Construction of Feeder Roads:

Planning work for slope land development was completed, and the projects for integrated soil conservation and land use improvement, utilization and care of released national forest lands and experimental regional development have been started since July 1973. Currently, construction of farm roads and irrigation facilities under the various projects is in progress, soil conservation work has been completed for 1,400 hectares, and assistance in farm management is already under way. Of the 22 feeder roads totalling 208 kilometers in length, one has already been completed, 14 are under construction and seven are in the stage of inviting bids from contractors.

Construction of Simple Waterworks in Rural Areas and Improvement of Environmental Sanitation:

As a measure to improve the living conditions in out-of-the-way, impoverished regions and specialized agricultural production areas, construction of simple waterworks by three separate stages in two years has been programmed for supplying water service to 222 villages with a total of 360,000 inhabitants. Improvement of environmental sanitation will be effected for 40 villages with some 50,000 inhabitants. Training in sanitary practice is conducted in each locality immediately after the completion of the engineering work.

Actual performance for the projects is as follows: Construction of eleven water supply systems for 24 villages and 33 others for another 117 villages was completed respectively in the first and second stages of the program. Meanwhile, improvement of environmental sanitation has been largely carried through for 10 villages. Villagers especially welcome projects for improvement of homes, including such facilities as kitchens, toilets and baths.

Projects for the promotion of agricultural development on the off-shore islands of Kinmen and Matsu implemented in 1973 numbered 21, entailing a total expenditure of NT$35 million. Most of these were for increase of food crops and improvement of irrigation facilities. Eleven small-sized dams have been installed in Kinmen, thus increasing irrigated areas by 100 hectares. The simple waterworks at Kinsha, Matsu, was completed and put into operation, now supplying water to over 300 homes.

Acceleration of the Extension of Integrated Use of Improved Cultural Techniques and Intensification of Efforts for Farm Mechanization:

The main purpose at extension of integrated use of improved cultural techniques consists in demonstrating the practice on an expanded scale so as to prove its advantages of giving larger unit area yield and bringing down the production cost. Not only the participants in the program will be benefited, but all other farmers in the neighboring areas may follow suit and thereby draw advantage from the program.

The extension work for the first stage involved 14,986 hectares of farmland scattered in 39 villages, with altogether 23,500 farm families participating. By the end of July 1973, this work was fully completed. The per hectare rice yield in areas covered by the program was 4,887 kilograms, 732 kilograms in excess of the 4,155 kilograms reaped from each hectare of other comparable farmland, which means an 18% increase in productivity. Production cost averaged NT$12,847 for farmlands covered by the program, NT$118 or 1% in excess of other comparable farmlands. The net income from farmlands covered by the program averaged NT$12,377, NT$3,649 or 42% in excess of other comparable farmlands.

To be covered in the second stage of the program will be 20,000 hectares of farmland in 49 villages in Toucheng. The emphasis of the work will be on the continuing of the practices introduced after the completion of the project, so that the techniques employed and benefits therefrom may be successfully retained.

Currently, 211 extension teams composed of 1,035 working groups are in operation. Paddies planted with seedlings totalled 20,680 hectares, of which 19,460 hectares are worked with farm machines. And cooperative pest and plant disease control has been introduced for 17,542 hectares of these lands.

Integrated cultural method has been practised on peanut crops in areas totalling 1,467 hectares during the first stage of the program. Production cost for these crops has been lowered by NT$633. For the second stage, 458 more hectares will be covered by the extension work.

Integrated use of cultural techniques has also been adopted for such summer/autumn crops as soybeans and sweet potatoes. It is expected that the per hectare yield will thereby be increased by 30%, with the total crops of soybeans and sweet potatoes increased respectively by 25,300 and 27,900 metric tons.

Important items of promotional work for farm mechanization during the first stage of the present program include: installation of large-sized paddy rice drying equipment, trial manufacture and demonstration of paddy rice combines, assistance to small farmers participating in collective farming, encouragement of the organization of mechanized farm service teams, training in the use of farm machines, and experimentation with the use of large-sized rice harvestors on an expanded scale.

Large drying equipment, combines and harvestors are still in the experimentation stage, and full benefit of their use may be realized gradually in the long run.

Up to date, 260 mechanized farm service teams have been set up with government financial support. Farmlands cultivated by these teams totalled 14,000 hectares. For the second stage of the program, three sets of large-sized drying equipment have been procured, and the use of rice combines, now coming out of the stage of engineering, will be actively extended. Meanwhile, 49 new farm mechanization instructors have been fostered and 26 farm machine utilization classes, with a total of 639 farmer-trainees, have been held. All these will facilitate the progress of the farm mechanization program.

Establishment of Specialized Agricultural Production Areas:

Establishment of 17 kinds of specialized agricultural production areas (among which are those for upland food crops, silk, tea, fruits, vegetables, flowers, bamboo shoots, livestock, and fish culture) involving a total expenditure of NT$147 million has been successfully promoted during the first stage

of the program. About 65% of the spending was for the construction of roads, products collecting centers, irrigation facillties and storehouses and procurement of pesticide spraying equipment and farm machines.

During the first stage of the program, 14 kilometers of road, 49 collecting centers with a total area of 3,100 *ping*, and 247 installations and 18 kilometers of ditches for irrigation were constructed. To meet the needs in the specialized production areas, tractors, harvestors, powered tillers and powered sprayers were procured; milk collection stations, artificial insemination centers and water supply systems were set up, and land consolidation was carried out. All these measures have helped lower production and marketing costs, and constitute the groundwork for promotion of regional development.

As to the methods of sale of farm produce, contract arrangements are generally adopted for seedless watermelons, garlics, green asparagus and silk cocoons; sales price guarantees are provided for corn, soybeans, millet and milk; and the Provincial Farmers' Association, fruit cooperatives or processing plants of hogs, bananas and tea make purchases at market prices. Meanwhile, to facilitate the operation of specialized production areas, joint marketing has been introduced for such products as vegetables and hogs. Farmers benefiting from this practice are estimated at 29,000, having realized additional incomes totalling some NT$20 million.

Encouragement of the Establishment of Factories in Rural Areas:

This project is aimed at increasing job opportunities available to the rural people and enhancement of the value added of the farm produce. Its benefits are far-reaching and long-lasting.

During the first stage of the program, two industrial districts, one occupying 22 hectares and other occupying 16 hectares, were opened up, respectively at Chushan, Nantou, and Yuanchang, Yunlin. Development of the districts is well in progress, with public facilities largely completed. The Chushan industrial district will be specialized in bambooware manufacture for export purposes, with the raw material supplied from some 10,000 hectares of bamboos in its neighborhood. The Yuanchang industrial district, on the other hand, is for labor-intensive processing plants of various kinds. Some 7,500 workers will be employed in each of these two districts when they start operation.

Strengthening of Agricultural Research and Extension:

Research and experimentation is a long-term investment, returns from which are often long in coming.

During the first stage of the program, designing of deep-sea fishery research vessels was accom-plished. The Taiwan Machinery Manufacturing Corporation has been granted a contract for construction of one such vessel at an estimated cost of NT$50 million. It will, after its completion, take up the task of pioneering for the nation's deep-sea fisheries.

The improved variety of tilapia has been successfully extended with some 7,650,000 fry breeded and supplied to fish farmers. Because the grown-up fish of the improved variety sells for NT$10 more a kilogram than the original variety, the improved variety finds a warm welcome among the farmers. It is estimated that the new fish will bring the farm in an additional income of NT$15,300,000.

The emergency hog disease prevention program was wound up successfully. Hogs given anti-cholera inoculation totalled 700,000 head, with the result that incidence of hog cholera was lowered by a half in the first six months of 1972 as compared with that in the same period of 1971. This has greatly diminished the possible loss of the hog farmers and eventually helps increase the production of hogs.

For the second stage, main efforts will be directed at increasing research and experimentation facilities and development of new food processing techniques and new food products. The expenses involved will amount to NT$97 million, the largest outlay ever provided for agricultural research and experimentation.

INDUSTRIAL PRODUCTION

The economic development strategy adopted by the Republic of China in the past was to foster a balanced development between agriculture and industry by making each of the two major economic sectors conducive to the growth of the other. However, as a result of the accelerated pace of industrial development in the last few years, the economic structure has undergone a change whereby industry has come to the fore to replace agriculture as the mainstay of the economy.

The growth rate of industrial production averaged 20% between 1966 and 1973. The growth has continued at a high speed following the termination of U.S. economic aid in 1965, an indication that the industry of Taiwan has attained a self-sustaining stage of development.

INDUSTRIAL PRODUCTION INDICES

The indices cover four sectors, namely, mining, manufacturing, construction and public utilities. They were compiled on the basis of 273 items of commodities and services. Taking 1966 as the base year, the 1973 general index for industry as a whole rose to 369.4. Among the group indices of 1973, the highest was manufacturing's 401.2. It was followed by construction's 395.3, public utilities' 281.0 and mining's 110.7.

Output of Principa

Item	Coal	Natural Gas	Sugar	Cotton Yar
Year	(M/T)	(1000m³)	(M/T)	(M/T)
1961	4,236,574	37,069	851,856	48,910
1962	4,553,581	38,397	686,363	52,448
1963	4,810,040	50,653	722,828	48,056
1964	5,027,653	169,394	903,306	50,546
1965	5,054,463	309,676	967,987	54,936
1966	5,014,533	439,168	927,304	59,759
1967	5,078,403	527,157	801,925	70,280
1968	5,014,328	704,453	770,124	69,595
1969	4,645,454	893,499	660,494	78,791
1970	4,473,467	918,043	653,063	87,223
1971	4,096,594	1,090,773	733,579	105,241
1972	3,913,218	1,263,857	752,225	91,362
1973	3,327,107	1,454,303	791,908	97,262

Industrial Production Indices

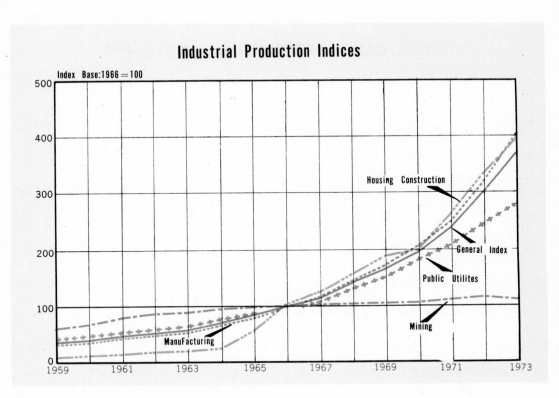

Index Base:1966 = 100

Housing Construction
General Index
Public Utilites
Mining
ManuFacturing

Industrial Products

austic Soda (M/T)	Chemical Fertilizer (M/T)	Sheet Glass (Std. Case)	Cement (M/T)	Aluminum Ingots (M/T)	Electric Power (1,000KWH)
36,479	270,203	446,189	1,509,588	9,017	4,083,707
37,913	366,540	504,368	1,870,411	11,009	4,692,662
45,338	443,937	411,999	2,245,960	11,929	4,018,536
57,472	735,301	582,246	2,355,246	19,372	5,914,078
62,436	897,905	703,776	2,443,654	18,911	6,455,424
73,634	915,684	831,569	3,114,713	17,216	7,340,161
88,495	996,532	1,620,158	3,486,812	15,440	8,412,337
91,011	1,102,484	1,781,012	3,993,369	20,020	9,802,235
107,196	1,193,983	1,948,660	4,088,350	22,108	11,118,735
126,201	1,087,324	1,935,707	4,304,801	26,991	13,212,851
134,561	1,036,783	1,772,124	5,042,947	26,546	15,170,917
151,906	1,169,569	2,187,351	5,689,503	32,104	17,449,264
238,715	1,293,992	2,275,778	5,974,997	35,111	19,804,987

AGRICULTURAL PRODUCTION

Agricultural productivity in Taiwan has increased tremendously as a result of successful experimentation, betterment of farming techniques, accumulation of agricultural investment and the strengthening of agricultural organizations. The annual growth in agriculture averaged 3.8 percent during the 1966-73 period. The steady expansion of agricultural production has been an important contributing factor to the fast growth in the industrial sector.

AGRICULTURAL PRODUCTION INDICES

The indices cover 139 items in four areas-agriculture, forestry, fisheries and livestock. Whith 1966 as the base year, the 1973 indices were 194.3 for fish catch, 183.7 for livestock, 111.6 for foestry products, and 109.1 for farm crops, the general agricultural index of the year being 126.3.

AGRICULTURAL OUTPUT

Since the area of arable land in Taiwan can not be expanded to any considerable extent, emphasis must be placed on increase of productivity. Factors contributing to such an increase are the introduction of new plant varieties, the improvement of cultivation techniques, effective pest control, extension of integrated farming programs and betterment of irrigation systems. Take rice for example, production increased from 1,642,000 M/T in 1953 to 2,255,000 M/T in 1973, registering a gain of 37%, without any sizable increase in land under cultivation. Output of other crops also showed substantial increases.

With regard to livestock production, efforts have been directed to promotion of integrated hog-raising program and use of mountain slopes for dairy farms. Hog production rose from 1,632,000 head in 1953 to 5,804,000 (number slaughtered) in 1973, an increase of 2.6 times. The number of fowls grew from 22 million in 1953 to 56 million in 1973, an increase of 1.5 times.

Deep-sea fishery has set the pace for other fisheries. By 1973, there were 1,293 fishing craft engaged in deep-sea fishing. They operated in the Indian, Atlantic and South Pacific Oceans from 55 overseas bases and supply harbors. Fishery production went upward from 131,000 M/T in 1953 to 759,000 M/T in 1973, showing an increase of over 4.8 times.

Timber production increased from 463,000 cubic meters in 1953 to 1,100,000 cubic meters in 1973, an increase of 1.4 times.

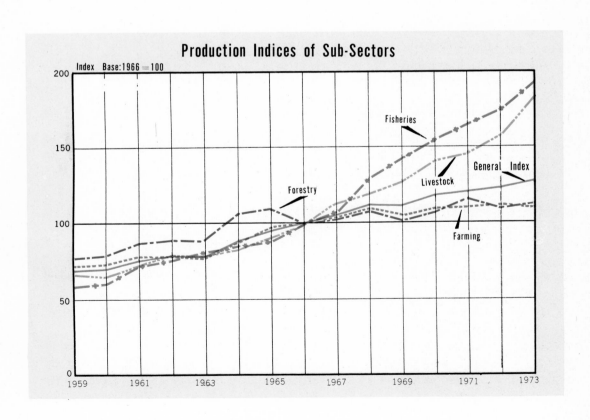

Output of Principal Farm Products

Unit: Metric ton

Year	Rice	Sweet Potatoes	Bananas	Pineapple	Peanuts	Citrus Fruits	Tea	Mush-rooms	Aspara-gus	
1956	1,789,829	2,568,104	58,696	83,065	81,847	35,332	13,420	—	—	98,985
1957	1,839,009	2,693,417	92,466	98,916	93,714	38,954	15,002	—	—	91,699
1958	1,894,127	2,957,893	111,266	136,859	96,423	41,835	15,764	—	—	99,554
1959	1,856,316	2,894,146	104,474	145,923	97,042	42,567	16,507	—	—	84,538
1960	1,912,018	2,978,676	114,216	166,730	102,167	52,866	17,365	—	—	73,401
1961	2,016,276	3,233,563	129,669	173,547	104,644	54,927	18,064	2,784	—	80,253
1962	2,112,874	3,079,586	140,875	192,307	95,496	67,141	19,753	12,875	—	91,300
1963	2,109,037	2,148,172	132,489	163,307	91,438	78,680	21,104	33,639	—	133,231
1964	2,246,639	3,347,797	267,898	226,682	115,727	102,341	18,306	22,718	616	124,477
1965	2,348,042	3,131,103	460,094	231,005	125,817	114,434	20,730	32,430	16,776	132,437
1966	2,379,661	3,460,106	527,721	270,389	114,995	136,695	21,510	33,454	44,120	107,251
1967	2,413,789	3,719,945	653,800	296,081	136,999	155,324	24,403	50,181	31,010	80,360
1968	2,518,103	3,444,619	645,467	311,364	106,489	175,578	24,418	52,400	51,583	58,251
1969	2,321,633	3,701,769	585,531	325,013	100,764	170,105	26,248	32,814	82,431	52,470
1970	2,462,643	3,440,639	461,829	338,191	122,198	209,115	27,648	39,021	112,331	56,925
1971	2,313,802	3,391,354	470,595	358,529	97,579	253,149	26,984	57,422	127,517	40,352
1972	2,440,329	2,927,708	366,411	334,384	94,032	290,609	26,229	85,528	106,602	38,448
1973	2,254,730	3,203,778	422,546	379,482	97,933	331,714	28,639	64,299	112,477	31,112

FOREIGN TRADE

Surrounded by seas on all sides, Taiwan is an insular economy not richly endowed by nature. External trade is therefore an essential means for ensuring an adequate supply of resources. Over the years, the Government's trade promotion efforts, particulary in regard to export expansion, have been highly fruitful, with the result that the Taiwan economy has been enjoying a sustained prosperity. The following is a brief review of the nation's trade development in recent years based on the statistics of the Inspectorate-General of Customs, Ministry of Finance:

Foreign trade has been making enormous gains since 1952. Commodity exports in 1973 totalled US$4,483,000,000, an increase of US$4,367,000,000 or 38 times over 1952's US$116,000,000. Commodity imports totalled US$3,793,000,000, an increase of US$ 3,606,000,00 or 19 times over 1952's US$-187,000 000. As revealed by these statistics, the nation's export trade expanded at a faster pace than its import trade between 1971 and 1973, with the consequence that export surpluses were registered successively over the years.

Value of Total Imports & Exports

Base: 1966 = 100   Unit for Value: US$1,000

Year	Exports			Imports		
	Value of Exports	Value Index	Quantum Index	Value of Imports	Value Index	Quantum Index
1952	116,474	6.84	23.35	187,215	10.15	30.22
1953	127,608	9.25	35.04	191,700	11.04	37.33
1954	93,299	6.76	24.23	211,433	13.24	39.23
1955	123,275	8.94	30.11	201,022	12.61	36.48
1956	118,296	13.66	29.10	193,696	19.23	35.10
1957	148,285	17.13	33.89	212,243	21.07	37.91
1958	155,814	18.00	41.34	226,188	22.46	42.31
1959	156,906	26.61	38.98	231,441	33.74	46.77
1960	163,982	27.81	38.25	296,780	43.26	51.76
1961	195,158	36.42	39.39	322,116	51.67	56.33
1962	218,206	40.72	44.84	304,110	48.76	56.51
1963	331,665	61.92	55.56	361,636	58.03	65.28
1964	432,956	80.94	73.03	427,968	68.76	74.49
1965	449,682	83.85	83.21	556,011	89.34	94.53
1966	536,270	100.00	100.00	622,361	100.00	100.00
1967	640,730	119.48	116.09	805,832	129.48	128.57
1968	789,189	147.16	142.40	903,280	145.14	144.89
1969	1,049,365	195.18	181.64	1,212,698	194.85	194.44
1970	1,428,293(1,487,436)	266.34	239.32	1,523,951	244.87	239.72
1971	1,997,661(2,060,393)	372.51	325.22	1,843,938	296.28	273.02
1972	2,916,212(2,988,123)	543.80	436.75	2,513,503	403.87	331.98
1973	4,395,584(4,483,366)	780.31	527.77	3,792,496	581.32	388.02

Remark: Figures in parenthesis including sales proceeds or fish catches overseas and petroleum products at the harbors.

Category / Year	Total Value	%	Category 0 Value	%	Category 1 Value	%	Category 2 Value	%	Category Value	
1961	8,347	100	657	7.88	1,122	13.45	483	5.79	1,524	1
1962	9,155	100	907	9.92	928	10.13	304	3.33	1,226	1
1963	11,312	100	1,485	13.12	1,108	9.80	266	2.35	2,153	1
1964	15,354	100	2,411	15.70	1,197	7.79	422	2.75	2,280	1
1965	19,754	100	2,741	13.87	911	4.61	355	1.80	2,230	1
1966	24,957	100	3,802	15.23	1,988	7.97	556	2.23	3,130	1
1967	32,314	100	5,415	16.76	1,439	4.45	772	2.23	3,707	1
1968	36,222	100	6,588	18.20	2,457	6.78	722	1.99	4,138	1
1969	48,629	100	8,322	17.14	2,508	5.15	949	1.95	5,514	1
1970	61,108	100	10,804	17.68	2,769	4.53	1,259	2.06	7,255	1
1971	73,942	100	11,495	15.55	3,057	4.13	1,525	2.06	9,195	1
1972	100,791	100	17,152	17.02	7,630	7.57	1,894	1.88	10,453	1
1973	145,079	100	26,672	13.38	4,928	3.40	2,337	1.61	15,372	1

Category / Year	Total Value	%	Category 0 Value	%	Category 1 Value	%	Category 2 Value	%	Category Value	
1961	7,812	100	791	10.12	169	2.17	3,792	48.54	1,748	2
1962	8,735	100	749	8.57	125	1.43	3,497	40.03	2,540	2
1963	13,283	100	1,165	8.77	120	0.91	6,394	48.14	3,232	24
1964	17,362	100	1,886	10.86	179	1.03	8,108	46.70	4,302	24
1965	17,987	100	2,676	14.87	156	0.87	7,043	39.16	4,714	2
1966	21,451	100	3,156	14.72	166	0.78	6,496	30.28	6,362	2
1967	25,629	100	3,196	12.47	171	0.67	6,652	25.95	8,742	3
1968	31,788	100	3,078	9.68	177	0.56	6,923	21.78	12,412	3
1969	41,975	100	3,506	8.35	144	0.34	7,426	17.69	17,066	4
1970	57,132	100	3,539	6.19	92	0.16	7,714	13.50	25,015	4
1971	79,906	100	4,765	5.96	56	0.07	9,386	11.75	37,220	4
1972	116,648	100	5,684	4.87	69	0.06	12,492	10.70	50,929	4
1973	167,383	100	7,659	4.58	233	0.14	16,436	9.82	67,544	4

Remarks:

Category 0: farm products, forestry products, livestock products, fishery products, and hunting products; Category 1: coal, metal ores, crude oil and natural gas, sand and gravel, crude salt, and non-metallic minerals; Category 2: fresh and preserved meat, canned and preserved fruits, vegetables and sea foods, grain mill products, bakery products, sugar and sugar preparations, miscellaneous food preparations, beverage and tobacco products; Category 3: textile products, leather, leather and fur products (except footwear and other wearing apparel), wood and cork products (except furniture), knitted and crocheted articles, footwear, wearing apparel, furniture, pulp, paper and allied products, printed matter and allied products and rubber products; Category 4: petroleum refinery products, products of petroleum and coal (except petroleum refinery products), structure stone and others, glass and glass products, ceramics, cement and cement products and non-

Unit for Value: NT$ Million

Category 4		Category 5		Category 6		Category 7		Category 8		Category 9	
lue	%	Value	%	Value	%	Value	%	Value	%	Value	%
148	1.77	1,474	17.66	1,057	12.66	1,625	19.46	197	2.36	60	0.71
202	2.20	1,944	21.23	1,253	13.68	2,062	22.52	263	2.88	66	0.72
139	1.23	1,740	15.38	1,360	12.02	2,758	24.38	254	2.25	49	0.44
221	1.44	2,697	17.57	2,007	13.07	3,696	34.07	354	2.31	69	0.45
551	3.30	3,132	15.86	3,064	15.51	6,069	30.72	507	2.57	94	0.47
413	1.65	3,427	13.73	3,209	12.86	7,786	31.20	562	2.25	84	0.34
544	1.99	4,562	14.12	3,632	11.24	11,357	35.15	709	2.19	127	0.39
523	1.72	4,597	12.69	3,397	9.38	12,789	35.31	766	2.10	145	0.40
739	1.52	6,457	13.28	4,273	8.78	18,593	38.23	1,098	2.25	176	0.36
913	1.49	7,551	12.36	6,005	9.83	22,757	37.24	1,525	2.50	270	0.44
408	1.90	10;159	13.74	7,727	10.45	26,729	36.15	2,028	2.74	619	0.84
316	1.80	13,629	13.52	9,588	9.51	35,031	34.76	2,594	2.57	1,004	1.00
509	1.73	20,662	14.24	15,093	10.40	51,760	35.68	4,155	2.86	1,591	1.10

Unit for Value: NT$ Million

ategory 4		Category 5		Category 6		Category 7		Category 8		Category 9	
lue	%	Value	%	Value	%	Value	%	Value	%	Value	%
300	3.84	445	5.70	365	4.67	150	1.92	51	0.65	1	0.01
520	5.96	636	7.29	347	3.97	209	2.39	111	1.27	1	0.01
674	5.08	686	5.16	526	3.96	361	2.70	124	0.93	1	0.01
743	4.28	730	4.20	566	3.26	571	3.29	261	1.51	16	0.09
541	3.01	808	4.49	654	3.64	994	5.53	382	2.12	19	0.10
956	4.92	878	4.09	832	3.88	1,953	9.10	524	2.44	28	0.13
262	4.92	1,129	4.41	882	3.44	2,712	10.58	829	3.24	54	0.21
170	3.68	958	3.01	720	2.26	4,670	14.69	1,608	5.06	72	0.23
120	2.67	1,222	2.91	1,255	2.99	7,190	17.13	2,973	7.08	73	0.18
335	2.34	1,425	2.50	2,607	4.56	10,873	19.03	4,470	7.82	62	0.11
576	2.10	1,529	1.91	2,358	2.95	15,716	19.67	7,133	8.93	67	0.08
020	1.74	1,829	1.57	3,941	3.38	28,163	24.14	11,381	9.76	140	0.12
571	1.60	2,459	1.47	2,990	1.79	42,597	25.45	24,613	14.70	181	0.10

metallic mineral products; Category 5: chemical elements and compounds, chemicals from petroleum and coal, dyeing, tanning and coloring materials, medicinal and pharmaceutical products, essential oils, perfume materials and toilet preparations, chemical fertilizer, explosives and pyrotechnic products, plastic materials, regenerated cellulose and artificial resins, and other chemical materials and products; Category 6: iron and steel, and non-ferrous metals; Category 7: metal products (except machinery and transportation equipment), machinery (except electric machinery), electric machinery and equipment and supplies, and transportation equipment; Category 8: professional and scientific measuring and controlling instruments, photographic and optical goods, watches and clocks, jewellery and related articles, musical instruments and other manufactured goods; Category 9: electricity, water and gas, works of art, collectors' pieces and antiques, miscellaneous goods other than agricultural, mining and manufacturing products.

MAJOR TRADING PARTNERS:

Buyers of Taiwan's Exports:

The Republic of China's exports reached more than 100 countries and areas in 1973. The United States, which imported US$1,677,072,000 from Taiwan (37.4% of the nation's total commodity exports in the year), was the leading buyer. Japan ranked second by importing US$824,152,000 (18.4% of the total). Other important buyers were, in order of importance, Hongkong (importing US$295,840,000 or 6.6%), West Germany (US$215,277,000 or 4.8%), Canada (US$170,962,000 or 3.8%), Singapore (US$-129,560,000 or 2.9%), Indonesia (US$118,280,000 or 2.6%), United Kingdom (US$112,246,000 or 2.5%), Australia (US$107,764,000 or 2.4%), Holland (US$-89,172,000 or 2.0%), Thailand (US$63,777,000 or 1.4%), Republic of Korea (US$53,546,000 or 1.2%), Malaysia (US$30,941,000 or 0.7%), Vietnam (US$-29,290,000 or 0.7%),the Philippines (US$28,969,000 or 0.7%), Saudi Arabia (US$24,930,000 or 0.6%), Kuwait (US$24,117,000 or 0.5%), Republic of South Africa (US$12,557,000 or 0.3%), and other countries and areas (US$474,914,000 or 10.5%).

Suppliers of Imports:

In 1973, the Republic of China imported goods from over 60 countries and areas. Japan, the largest supplier, sold US$1,427,697,000 worth of goods (37.7% of the nation's total commodity imports of the year) to Taiwan. It was followed by the United States, from which US$952,533,000 worth of goods .(25.1% of the total) was imported. Other major suppliers were, in order of importance, West Germany (US$203,276,000 or 5.4%). Australia (US$101,291,000 or 2.7%), Indonesia (US$ 101,181,000 or 2.7%), Hongkong (US$99,542,000 or 2.6%), United Kingdom (US$73,187,000 or 1.9%), Malaysia (US$62,028,000 or 1.6%), Kuwait (US$59,123,000 or 1.6%), Thailand (US$56,788,000 or 1.5%), the Philippines (US$-55,283,000 or 1.5%), Saudi Arabia (US$42,492,000 or 1.1%), Republic of Korea (US$41,995,000 or 1.1%), Holland (US$41,842,000 or 1.1%), Republic of South Africa (US$32,221,000 or 0.9%), Canada (US$-27,979,000 or 0.7%), SinꞬapore (US$26,587,000 or 0.7%), Vietnam (US$5,983,000 or 0.2%), and other countries and areas US$380,468,000 or 9.9%).

INTERNATIONAL TECHNICAL COOPERATION

To the Republic of China, international technical cooperation has been a two-way business. It has been rendering technical services to friendly countries while itself receiving foreign technical assistance.

TECHNICAL SERVICES FOR FOREIGN COUNTRIES:

Technical assistance is rendered to foreign countries by the Republic of China by means of: (a) invitation of economic development officials of cooperating nations to come to Taiwan to observe the development projects undertaken and economic progress made here, (b) dispatch of Chinese specialists to make an inspection of a cooperating country to identify opportunities for bilateral cooperation and map out the cooperation program; (c) dispatch of Chinese technicians to cooperating countries to demonstrate the Chinese industrial and or agricultural production methods and practices (e.g., farm demonstration teams and other technical missions), and (d) invitation of foreign technicians to attend seminars and training courses here.

From 1954 through 1973, 7,379 specialists from 23 countries came to the Republic of China for technical training under the U.S. Aid-financed technical assistance program.

Foreign Participants in Training Conducted in the Republic of China Under Various Technical Cooperation Programs

From 1954 to 1973   Unit: Person

Country	Total	Agriculture	Industry	Transpor-tation	Health & Sanitation	Education	Public Adm.	Community Development	Labor	General & Misc.
Grand Total	7,379	3,348	557	68	1,187	1,009	802	349	12	47
Afghanistan	5				5					
Brazil	1	1								
Khmer	16	4			3					9
Ceylon	2	2								
Dahomey	4							4		
Ethiopia	5	1			2	2				
Indonesia	2							2		
Iran	5	5								
Japan	25	25								
Republic of Korea	449	137	60	7	119	39	62	25		
Laos	38	17				21				
Malagasy Republic	2	2								
Micronesia	2	2								
Nepal	4	1	2			1				
Pakistan	1	1								
Peru	2					2				
Philippines	575	341	17			104	70	8	31	4
Ryukyu	1,406	538	285	9	119	197	238			20
Sierra Leone	2							2		
Thailand	2,664	1,269	77	8	485	339	191	285	3	7
Turkey	12	12								
Vietnam	2,154	987	116	44	349	341	303		9	7
Guyana	3	3								

As a developing country that has made remarkable progress in recent years, the Republic of China is providing technical services to a number of friendly developing nations that have shown an interest in its development experience and requested its assistance in their own development efforts. While farm demonstration to introduce rice culture techniques is a major field of activity of Chinese technicians working overseas, technical services have also been rendered to friendly countries in Africa, Latin America, Southeast Asia and other parts of the world in various other fields including water conservancy, medical service, highway engineering, fisheries, farmers' organization, livestock industry, irrigation, paper manufacture, textiles, chemical engineering, quality control, industrial research and pharmacy. Up to the end of 1973, a total of 2,928 agricultural technicians had been sent abroad to work on the vavious farm demonstration teams and some 300 other specialists, to render technical services in other fields. Their highly gratifying performance has helped strengthen the ties of friendship and amity with many other free countries.

To provide African agricultural technicians with in-service training, agricultural seminars have been regularly held in Taiwan since 1962. Up to the end of 1973, altogether 683 agriculturists from over 30 African nations had participated in the seminars. And in order to share with other developing countries the knowledge and experience of this nation in promotion of land reform, the Chinese Government, in conjunction with the Lincoln foundation of the United States, set up a Land Reform Training Center in Taoyuan County in 1969, which has since conducted land reform courses for 613 trainees from 29 countries.

In addition, the Republic of China has set up a number of research and training agencies under different regional and international cooperation programs. Among these are the Asia Food and Fertilizer Technology Center established with the support of the Asian and Pacific Council and the Asian Vegetable Research and Development Center launched jointly by the Chinese Government and the U.S. Agency for International Development with the support of the Republic of Korea, Thailand, the Philippines and Japan. With the cooperation of the American Population Council, the Taiwan Provincial Government has in operation a Chinese Center for International Training in Family Planning which is training foreign as well as Chinese medical workers in promotion of family planning.

TECHNICAL ASSISTANCE FROM FOREIGN COUNTRIES:

Foreign technical assistance received by the Republic of China comes generally under two categories: technical knowledge that the nation is urgently in need of acquired by competent technicians sent to advanced countries for on-the-job training or advanced studies; and the experience and expertise of foreign specialists to assist in efforts for tackling of technical or institutional problems being confronted or to help the nation with its research and planning work.

During the period from 1951 through 1973, a total of 3,132 technicians and specialists were sent abroad for studies and training under the U.S. aid-financed Joint Technical Assistance Committee (JTAC) programs. Another 5,472 went abroad for studies or training through assistance from various other sources, including 847 under U.N. technical assistance program, 316 under the sponsorship of the

Asian Productivity Organization, and 947, 181, 24, 20 and 5 under programs financed by the governments and private institutions of Japan, West Germany, Australia, France and Holland respectively.

Over the years, foreign specialists under the various foreign and international technical assistance programs totalled 1,106, including 102 financed by U.S. AID and its predecessor programs, 346 by U.N. technical assistance program, 66 by Asian Productivity Oranization, 104 by Sino-American Fund for Economic and Social Development, 130 by International Executive Corps, 43 by International Management Cooperation Committee, 272 by Japan, 23 by West Germany, 12 by Australia, 1 by France, and 7 by Italy.

Training of Chinese Technicians and Specialists under Various Technical Cooperation Programs

Category / Year	Total	Agriculture & Natural Resources	Industry & Mining	Communications & Transportation	Labor	Health & Sanitation	Education	Public Administration	Community Development & Social Work	Mass Communication & Others	Economic Development	Military Assistance
1951	49	18	5	1	0	8	13	1	0	3	0	0
1952	14	6	6	2	0	0	0	0	0	0	0	0
1953	167	50	44	18	0	27	7	19	0	0	0	2
1954	231	60	51	10	0	36	24	45	0	4	0	0
1955	239	48	32	12	0	17	59	13	1	11	0	46
1956	247	55	39	14	0	32	45	34	3	10	12	0
1957	241	73	57	14	0	22	34	15	0	12	14	0
1958	222	63	55	14	0	11	46	0	0	9	24	0
1959	271	62	61	29	0	5	58	21	0	4	31	0
1960	274	64	96	21	0	19	50	13	6	5	0	0
1961	187	66	19	9	0	15	44	20	0	10	4	0
1962	291	66	84	10	0	10	52	48	0	9	11	0
1963	252	44	108	8	0	3	36	37	0	12	4	0
1964	212	48	52	3	4	1	10	46	0	27	21	0
1965	195	27	71	14	13	0	4	31	1	30	4	0
1966	252	41	58	28	10	7	13	40	5	41	9	0
1967	261	58	53	22	7	7	28	23	8	42	13	0
1968	264	71	47	27	4	14	8	39	5	44	5	0
1969	269	49	68	21	7	16	15	36	5	40	12	0
1970	340	53	82	20	23	15	35	57	2	45	8	0
1971	364	42	69	22	16	21	43	64	24	44	19	0
1972	190	35	69	14	8	15	10	22	6	8	3	0
1973	118	13	30	8	14	3	17	21	4	8	—	0
Total	5150	1112	1256	341	111	304	651	645	70	418	194	48

Remarks: 322 persons sent abroad under U.N. technical assistance program between 1952 and 1962 have not been included in this tabulation for lack of detailed information.

TRANSPORTATION

RAILWAYS

Railways constitute the backbone of the transportation services on the island of Taiwan. With the exception of 1962, in which year the railway passenger traffic showed a slight decline as a consequence of the collection of defense surtax from the passengers, the railway traffic has been growing steadily over the years. In recent years, the average annual rate of increase in passenger service was 7.9%; that in freight service, 3.3%. The passenger traffic in 1973 was 8,017,596,000 passenger-kilometers, representing an increase of 3.2 times over 1,927,870,000 passenger-kilometers in 1952. The freight traffic in 1973 was 2,893,746,000 ton-kilometers, an increase of 1.3 times over 1,253,832,000 ton-kilometers in 1952. The average daily traffic of each kilometer of railway on Taiwan has now reached more than 400,000 passengers and 80,000 tons of freight. However, short-distance travelling and freight haul have been on the decrease in recent years in the face of the rapid development of highway transportation.

To cope with the growing demand for its services, the Taiwan Railway Administration will launch out into a project for electrification of the trunk railway of its West Line system, beside procuring more passenger and freight cars. Construction of the north bend railroad is under way and designs for an underground, rapid-transit system for Taipei City are in preparation.

HIGHWAY

Highway passenger service is provided by the Taiwan Highway Bureau and 25 private bus companies. The former operates a fleet of some 1,955 buses; the latter have a total of some 2,638 buses. Nine cities and counties are also served by their own local bus lines, whose buses number some 2,003. In addition, there are some 1,347 sightseeing buses in operation on the island.

Over the years, very rapid progress has been made in highway passenger service, with an 12.0% annual average growth in traffic in the past decade. The traffic volume in 1973 was 15,773,700,000 passenger kilometers, an increase of 9.5 times over 1,507,150,000 passenger-kilometers in 1952.

Highway-freight transportation is operated entirely by private trucking companies, which now number 1,523, having altogether some 17,010 trucks. The average annual rate of growth in the service of these trucking companies was 16.0% in the past decade. Their freight traffic in 1973 was 1,944,060,000 ton-kilometers, an increase of 29.5 times over

63,680,000 ton-kilometers in 1952.

The rapidly increasing traffic on the north-south mainline highway has resulted in frequent road congestions. Broadening of the bottleneck sections has afforded only little relief to the situation. The construction of a north-south freeway, which is the only adequate solution, is now under way, with completion scheduled for 1978.

AIR TRANSPORTATION

Taipei, an important midway station in the air route between the West Pacific and Southeast Asia, has seen rapid growth in air traffic in recent years. The average annual growth rate in the air passenger traffic during the past decade is 40%. In 1973, passengers arriving at and departing from the Taipei International Airport numbered 4,940,000; those stopping over in transit totalled 420,000. Freight handled at the airport in 1973 was 105,392 m.t. The daily arriving and departing flights averaged 236 in 1973, as compared with only 14 flights daily back in 1952. Meanwhile, keeping its pledge to fulfil the obligations imposed by the International Civil Aviation Organization to which the nation once belonged, the China Civil Aeronautics Administration has rendered highly reliable air navigational services to ensure air safety, a fact that has called forth widespread commendation.

With any further expansion of the Taipei airport prevented by its topographical features, the construction of a new international airport is under way in Taoyuan County. The work will be carried out in three stages. The first stage, to be completed in 1971-80, involves the building of runways, aprons and the terminal building and installation of navigational aid facilities.

SHIPPING

There are altogether 85 Chinese shipping companies, including the state-operated China Merchants Steam Navigation Co. and the Provincial Taiwan Navigation Corporation.

Back in 1952, the Chinese merchant fleet had only 132 vessels, totalling 4,650,000 dwt, which carried altogether 2,836,000 tons of freight. By the end of 1973, the fleet tonnage increased to 17,510,000 dwt, comprising 177 vessels; and the actual tonnage carried rose to 15,010,000 tons. The growth over the years was 290% in shipping tonnage, 34% in number of vessels and 430% in total tonnage carried.

Promotion of maritime shipping has been an unremitting endeavor of the Government for development of the Taiwan economy, inasmuch lower ocean freight means reduced costs of imported materials and supplies and also greater competitiveness of export goods in overseas markets. Moreover, shipping by national-flag vessels affords an appreciable saving in foreign exchange. Currently, liner services are provided by the Chinese merchant fleet between Taiwan and the U.S. East Coast, the U.S. West Coast, Japan, Southeast Asia and Europe. Unscheduled sailings to various parts of the world are also operated by a number of shipping companies.

HARBORS

Immediately after the Second World War, Keelung and Kaohsiung harbors were in a deplorable and nearly unserviceable state, with the fairways blocked by sunken ships and wharves and warehouses mostly destroyed by Allied bombings. Repairs done after the retrocession and the improvements and expansion of the harbor facilities subsequently brought about have led to a steady increase in the harbors' freight handling capacity. In East Taiwan, Hwalien Harbor was opened up as the island's third international harbor in September 1963 after years of development work.

The shipping traffic of the three harbors grew from 1952's 5,290,000 tons to 57,330,000 tons 1973, an increase of 9.8 times. Freight handled rose by 14 times from 1952's 3,300,000 m.t. to 49,280,000 m.t. in 1973.

To meet the urgent need for more port facilities resulting from the continued expansion of the nation's sea-borne commerce, planning for the construction of a new international harbor at Wuchi, Taichung, has been under way. With engineering work begun in 1973, the harbor will eventually have a freight handling capacity of 12,000,000 m.t.

TOURISM

Besides being an important economic factor, tourism is a useful medium for furtherance of a nation's efforts in a number of fields, including politics, culture, education, social work and intercommunication with the people of other nations. The tourist trade is therefore being actively promoted by most free world countries. Indeed, promotion of tourism is one of the grand-scale human endeavors of this modern world.

Development of the tourist trade did not begin on Taiwan until 1956. However, through the concerted efforts of the Government and the people, tourism facilities have steadily improved and expanded, and intensive and widespread promotion has brought on an ever-increasing tourist traffic. In 1973, visitors to this island numbered as many as 824,393.

A sampling survey of 1973 tourist traffic reveals that, on the average, each visitor spent US$64.98 per day or US$298.26 in 4.59 days, which was the average length of stay by the tourists. The total foreign exchange earnings of the tourist trade during the year amounted to US$245,882,000.

TRANSPORTATION

Railway & Highway Traffic

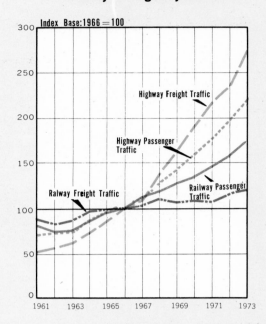

Index Base:1966 = 100

Highway Freight Traffic

Highway Passenger Traffic

Ralway Freight Traffic

Railway Passenger Traffic

Air & Marine Transportation

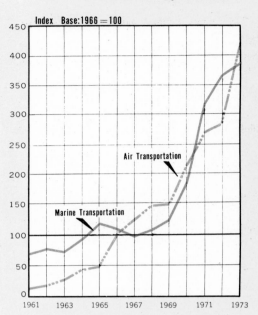

Index Base:1966 = 100

Air Transportation

Marine Transportation

Harbor Traffic

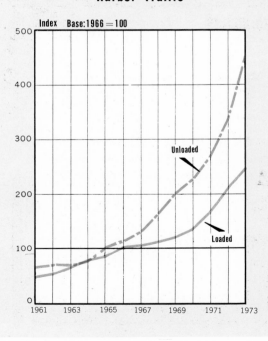

Index Base:1966 = 100

Unloaded

Loaded

Growth in Tourism

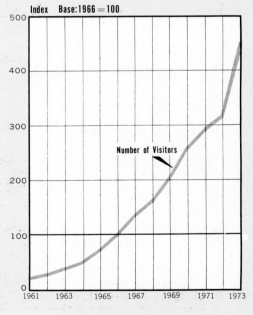

Index Base:1966 = 100

Number of Visitors

COMMUNICATIONS

POSTAL SERVICE

The volume of mail handled by the post offices in the Taiwan area increased in all years except 1960 and 1962, in which years slight decreases in mail were registered because of the upward readjustments made of the postal charges. Postal savings increased very rapidly in recent years as a consequence of continued economic boom.

Correspondence

A total of 62,290,000 pieces of correspondence was posted in 1952. The volume increased by 11.2 times to 762,650,000 pieces in 1973. The average annual rate of growth in the past decade was 8.3%.

Parcels

Parcels posted in 1952 numbered 430,000. The volume increased by 16.6 times to 7,580,000 by 1973. The average annual rate of growth in the past

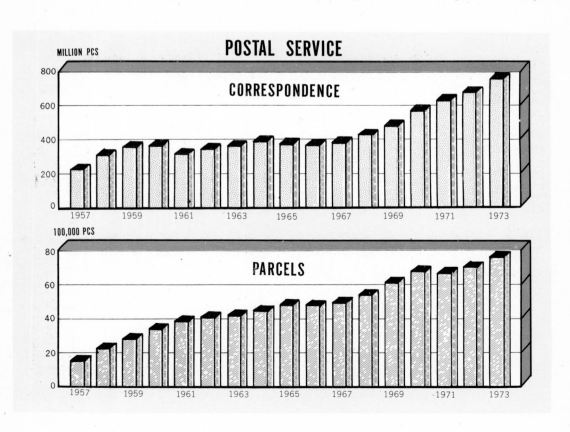

decade was 6.3%.

Postal Savings

Postal savings deposits at the end of 1952 amounted to NT$29,760,000. The amount rose to NT$17,745,610,000 in 1973, representing a gain of 595 times. The increase has been very fa since 1957, reflecting an accelerated growth in pe capita income and stable economic situation thenceforth. The average annual rate of increase in the past decade was 33.1%.

Remittances

Remittances increased by 49.8 times from NT$-245,410,000 in 1952 to NT$12,465,200,000 in 1973. The average annual rate of growth was 20.1%.

To save mailing time and avoid mail congestions, a program for mechanization of mail handling equipment is under way; and to better serve out-of-way rural areas, more post offices are being set up under a "one post office each village" program.

TELECOMMUNICATION

Telephone

There were 486,829 telephone subscribers in urban areas in 1973, representing an increase of 18.8 times compared with 1952 when the number of urban subscribers stood at 24,609. The average annual rate of increase in the number of subscribers in the past decade was 20.3%. The number of domestic long-distance telephone calls increased by 9.8 times from 1952's 4,775,856 to 51,761,033 in 1973. The average annual rate of growth in this service in the past decade was 11.4%. The number of international calls rose by 106 times from 1952's 19,553 to 2,095,845 in 1973. Its average annual rate of increase in the past decade was 18.5%.

Telegraph

With its annual traffic volume increased from 212,792 messages in 1952 to 2,568,028 messages in 1973, the domestic telegraphic service showed a growth of 11.1 times or an average annual growth of 13.8% in the past decade. The annual traffic volume of the international telegraphic service increased from 371,000 messages in 1952 to 1,690,633 messages in 1973, representing a growth 3.6 times of or an average annual growth of 12.7%.

The international telex service was inaugurated in Taipei in September 1960. In 1961, the volume of telex traffic was 3,885 minutes. It increased by 541 times to 2,105,624 minutes in 1973. The average annual rate of growth in the telex traffic in the past decade was 44.2%.

To coordinate with the rapid development of the economy and to meet national defense requirements, two trans-horizon microwave systems, namely, the Sino-Philippines and the Sino-Hong-kong-Vietnam, were completed in 1969 and 1970 respectively; a ground station for the Pacific region communications satellite was established in 1969, and construction of another one for the Indian Ocean area was completed in 1972. A plan for installation of long-distance dialing system is well under way.

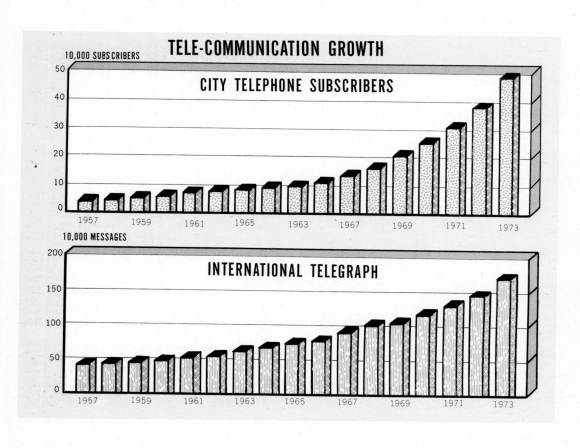

PUBLIC FINANCE, MONEY AND BANKING

GOVERNMENT REVENUE & EXPENDITURE

During the past 20 years, both government revenue and expenditure showed a steadily increasing tendency. While the absolute value of the difference between revenue and expenditure has been on the rise gradually, the ratio of the difference to the net expenditure has been on a downward trend.

Tax and monopoly revenue, which have always been the largest item of government revenue, accounted for 75.1% of the total government revenue in FY 1973. Earnings from business operations and income from enterprises constituted the second largest item, accounting for 10.7% of the total; and bond issues and loans, service or handling charges and fines, others, property sales and repossession followed in order, accounting for 4.4%, 3.8%, 3.8% and 1.9% respectively.

With regard to government expenditures, increased emphasis has been placed on welfare and economic development. Expenditures on education, science and culture, social affairs, relief and health, and reconstruction and communications have been rapidly increasing in recent years. In FY 1974, national defense and security accounted for 32.9% of the total expenditure of all levels of government; education, science and culture, 16.7% of the total; reconstruction and communications, 16.1%; social affairs, relief and health, 11.5%; public administration, 8.1%; reserve for adjustment of the pay of public servants and servicemen, 6.6%; debt servicing, 4.6%; and others, 3.5%.

MONEY & BANKING

From the changes in assets and liabilities of all financial institutions one can get a glimpse of the flow of funds between the financial sector and the other sectors in the Taiwan area.

The assets of all financial institutions include net foreign assets, claims against the Government, claims against public enterprises, and claims against private enterprises. The last mentioned have been increasing most rapidly, constituting the major item of outflow of funds from all financial institutions; the amount outstanding rose from NT$10.3 billion at end of 1961 to NT$176.7 billion at the end of 1973 (up by 16 times). Next came net foreign assets, which were only NT$5.2 billion at the end of 1961 and increased to NT$71.4 billion at the end of 1973, up by 12.7 times. Claims against the Government went up from NT$4.4 billion at the end of 1961 to NT$14.0 billion at the end of 1973, showing an increase of 2.2 times. Claims against public enterprises rose up from NT$5.8 billion at the end of 1961 to NT$27.2 billion at the end of 1973, an increase of 3.7 times.

The total outflow of funds from the financial institutions in 1973 amounted to NT$289.3 billion.

The liabilities of all financial institutions include money supply, government deposits, US aid deposits, and such quasi-money as time deposits, savings deposits and foreign currency deposits. Among them, quasi-money increased most rapidly: from NT$9.5 billion at the end of 1961 to NT$128.2 billion at the end of 1973 (up by 12.5 times), constituting the major item of inflow of funds to all financial institutions. Government deposits also increased very rapidly, from NT$2.4 billion at the end of 1961 to NT$438.7 billion at the end of 1973, showing a rise of 181.8 times. Money supply increased from NT$7.3 billion at the end of 1961 to NT$80.9 billion at the end of 1973. Other liabilities are shown in the accompanying table.

Consolidated Balance Sheet For All Financial Institutions

Unit: NT$ Million

Year	Assets					Liabilities					
	Total	Net foreign assets	Claims against Government	Claims against Public enterprises	Claims against private enterprises	Total	Total money Supply	Quasi-money	Government deposits	US-aid deposits	Net worth
1961	25,672	5,182	4,398	5,779	10,313	25,672	7,335	9,501	2,385	3,404	3,047
1962	29,691	4,480	4,516	7,431	13,264	29,991	7,923	12,145	2,980	3,955	2,688
1963	36,497	8,680	5,263	6,434	16,120	36,497	10,198	15,510	3,303	4,711	2,775
1964	45,339	11,292	6,061	7,316	20,670	45,339	13,431	19,720	3,644	5,614	2,930
1965	52,528	10,620	7,045	8,394	26,469	52,528	14,845	23,449	5,290	5,606	3,338
1966	62,716	13,410	8,832	9,375	31,099	62,716	17,393	29,517	8,009	4,309	3,488
1967	75,661	15,727	10,317	11,404	38,213	75,661	22,100	35,538	9,506	3,331	5,186
1968	86,604	14,011	11,760	12,415	48,418	86,604	24,890	39,978	13,347	1,842	6,547
1969	103,279	17,594	11,675	13,930	60,080	103,279	28,914	48,544	15,954	1,677	8,190
1970	124,733	24,915	12,395	16,273	71,150	124,733	35,085	60,755	18,446	1,364	9,083
1971	150,764	33,647	10,129	20,327	86,661	150,764	45,676	76,341	17,197	1,109	10,441
1972	209,043	58,341	10,011	22,895	117,796	209,043	55,066	105,359	22,750	1,729	24,139
1973	289,309	71,353	13,980	27,234	176,242	289,309	80,938	128,199	43,865	1,732	34,575

PUBLIC FINANCE, MONEY & BANKING

Government Revenue & Expenditure

FY 1974

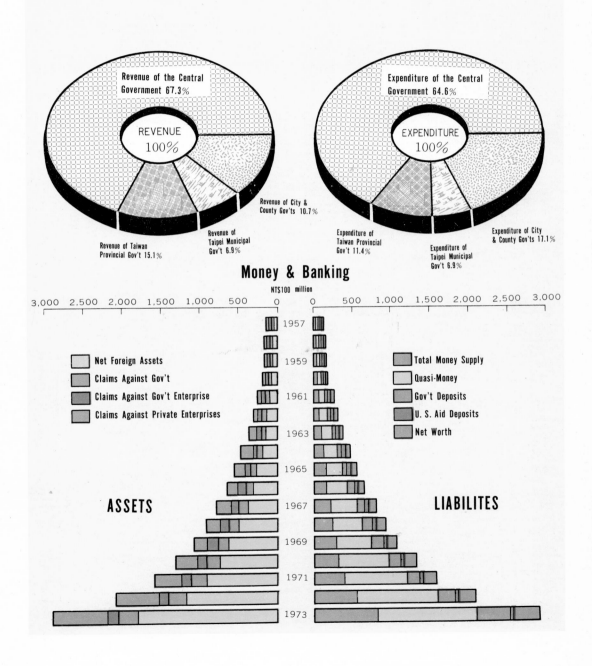

Revenue of the Central Government 67.3%

REVENUE 100%

Revenue of City & County Gov'ts 10.7%

Revenue of Taiwan Provincial Gov't 15.1%

Revenue of Taipei Municipal Gov't 6.9%

Expenditure of the Central Government 64.6%

EXPENDITURE 100%

Expenditure of Taiwan Provincial Gov't 11.4%

Expenditure of Taipei Municipal Gov't 6.9%

Expenditure of City & County Gov'ts 17.1%

Money & Banking

NT$100 million

3,000 2,500 2,000 1,500 1,000 500 0   0 500 1,000 1,500 2,000 2,500 3,000

Net Foreign Assets

Claims Against Gov't

Claims Against Gov't Enterprise

Claims Against Private Enterprises

Total Money Supply

Quasi-Money

Gov't Deposits

U. S. Aid Deposits

Net Worth

1957
1959
1961
1963
1965
1967
1969
1971
1973

ASSETS

LIABILITES

75

PRICE MOVEMENTS

The wholesale price indices and consumer price indices of major cities in Taiwan were compiled by the Directorate-General of Budget, Accounting & Statistics, Executive *Yuan*. Following is an analytical study of the wholesale and consumer prices of the last few years:

WHOLESALE PRICE INDICES

The general index of the wholesale prices covers a total of 586 items of commodities, which are divided into twelve different groups as follows: 132 in food, 65 in textile products, 40 in pharmaceuticals & herb medicines, 13 in leather & products, 16 in fuel & electric power, 6 in timber, 44 in building materials, 93 in metals & products, 17 in paper & pulp, 47 in chemicals & products, 18 in rubber & products and 95 in miscellaneous items.

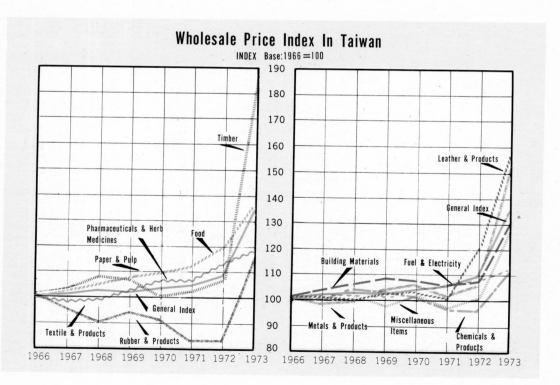

Wholesale Price Index In Taiwan
INDEX Base:1966=100

The general index of the wholesale prices, while trending upwards over the years, showed relatively moderate changes except in 1973. The Changes over the years were as follows: up 2.52% in 1967, up 1.99% in 1968, down 0.24% in 1969 up 2.72% in 1970, up 0.02% in 1971, up 4.65% in 1972, and up 22.86% in 1973.

A review of group indices:

In 1973, Taiwan's wholesale price index showed a very abrupt rise as a result of the impact of world inflation and the momentous change in the structure of the world economy and trade. Of the twelve groups of commodities covered by the general index, timber showed a rise of 74.93%; while the rise was 40.72% for metals, 39.57% for rubber & products, 32.30% for textiles products, 30.63% for leather & products, 30.33% for paper & pulp, 26.35% for miscellaneous items, 20.20% for building materials, 15.90% for chemicals & products, 15.68% for pharmaceuticals & herb medicines, 12.93% for food, and 4.37% for fuel.

CONSUMER PRICE INDICES OF MAJOR CITIES

Covered by the statistics on consumer prices are 298 items of goods and services which are divided into seven different groups: 108 in food, 44 in clothing, 53 in housing, 13 in communication services 36 in medicines & health care, 23 in education & recreation, and 21 in miscellaneous items.

The increases in the general index of consumer prices were 3.34% in 1967, 6.27% in 1968, 5.06% in 1969, 3.57% 1970, 2.56% in 1971, 4.85% in 1972, and 13.05% in 1973.

Of the seven groups of commodities covered

by the general index, food showed a rise of 13.94% while the rise was 24.90% for clothing, 11.97% for housing, 1.45% for communication services, 16.59% for medicines & health care, 11.23% for education & recreation, and 2.18% for miscellaneous items.

World monetary crisis and material shortage caused a sharp rise in the local price level in 1973. Meanwhile, the nation's export surpluses of the past years and the consequent expansion of money supply also acted as a stimulus to inflation. However, the Government's efforts to regulate commodity supply by making sufficient foreign exchange available for import of essential goods, in conjunction with the effective and timely financial and monetary measures, alleviated the rate of inflation.

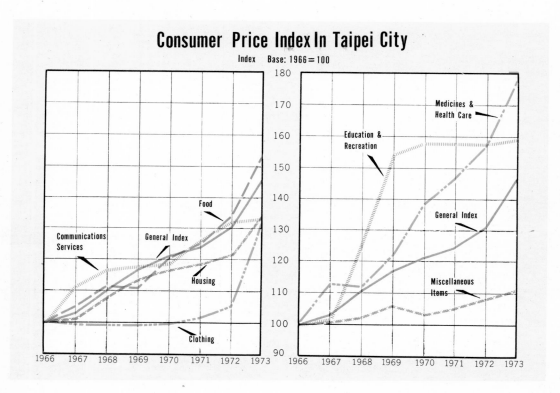

Consumer Price Index In Taipei City
Index   Base: 1966 = 100

MAJOR CONSTRUCTION PROJECTS

Ten major construction projects now under way or to be soon started include the nine embodied in the five-year infrastructure and heavy-chemical industries construction program announced by Premmier Chiang Ching-kuo on November 12, 1973, and the Taiwan Power Company's nuclear power generation project. The far-reaching effects these projects will have on Taiwan's economic future was clearly represented in what the Premier told a New York Times reporter in an interview on December 31, 1973: "Completion of the nine projects will enable this nation to rise from the status of a developing economy and win rank among the developed countries. Our Government has already laid out detailed plans for the nine projects with respect to their financing, the talents required and the construction materials needed. These projects are expected to be carried through in the next five years."

Given below is a brief description of each of the ten major projects:

North-South Superhighway:

To facilitate the flow of the island's rapidly increasing north-south overland traffic, a 373.4 kilometer superhighway extending from Keelung to Fengshan is now under construction. The project is to be carried out in three stages. The first stage, started in July 1971 and scheduled for completion in July 1974, covers the Keelung-Yangmei section. The second stage covers the construction of the Yangmei-Taichung and the Tainan-Fengshan sections and the third stage, that of the Taichung-Tainan section. The entire project is expected to complete in June 1978. Opening of this road to traffic will shorten the north-south travelling time from the present eight hours to a mere four hours. And it is estimated that, with the completion of this new road, the nation may save spending NT$70.2 billion on highway construction elsewhere during the next 20 years. The rate of return on the investment for this road is 20.25%.

Taichung Harbor Project:

The target of this project is to complete the construction of a commercial harbor of an annual freight handling capacity of 12,000,000 m.t. by 1982, with the necessary berthing facilities and an appendant fishing harbor simultaneously provided. The project will be carried out in three stages. The harbor will be capable of handling 2,800,000 m.t. of freight a year by 1976 after the completion of the first stage of the project started in 1973.

The construction of the harbor is aimed at relieving part of the traffic loads of Keelung and

Kaohsiung Harbors as well as the railroads and highways, and also a saving of overland transportation expenses. Another benefit of the project is the availability of a site for the establishment of a new industrial district on land newly reclaimed through the use of the mud dredged up from the barbor area. The internal rate of return of the project is estimated to be more than 25%.

North Bend (Suao-Hualien) Railroad

The North Bend Railroad will connect Nanhsinchen on the I-Lan Line to Tienpu on the East Line, with spur tracks leading to Hualien Harbor. The 88-kilometer railroad will pierce through mountains and cross over gorges and ravines, and therefore 43.3% of its total length will be bridges and tunnels.

The project will be carried out in two stages. The first stage, started in January 1974 and scheduled for completion in December 1975, will construct the Nanhsinchen-Tungao section in the north and the Hsincheng-Putien section in the south. The intermediate Tungao-Hsincheng section will be constructed in the second stage which will begin on July 1974 and end in December 1978.

The benefits of the project will be: Completion of a rail system serving both the west and east of the island, attraction of more shipping to Hualien Harbor, lightening of the traffic load of Keelung and Kaohsiung Harbors, and facilitation of the development of the natural resources in East Taiwan.

Electrification of the West Trunk Line of the Taiwan Railway:

Altogether 1,153 kilometers of railroad between Keelung and Kaohsiung (including 922 kilometers of mainlines and 231 kilometers of sidings) will be electrified. The implemention of the project will be divided into three stages. Electrification of the Keelung-Chunan section, which is to constitute the first stage, will be started in January 1975 and completed in December 1976; that of the Mountain and Coastal Lines between Chunan and Changhua, which is to constitute the second stage, will be started in March 1976 and completed in December 1977; that of Changhua-Kaohsiung section, which is to constitute the third stage, will be started in March 1977 and completed in December 1978.

The benefits of the project will be: Increase of the road capacity, shortening of the train running time by one-third, lowering of transportation cost, and furtherance of economic development efforts.

Taoyuan International Airport:

To cope with the rapid increase of civil air traffic, a new international airport will be constructed in Taoyuan, about 29 kilometers from Taipei. It is aimed at handling an annual air traffic of 5,000,000 passengers and 200,000 m.t. of freight and accommodating simultaneously 26 airplanes. The project will be started in July 1974 and completed in December 1978. The benefits of the project will be: Meeting of the excess traffic demand on Sungshan International Airport, furtherance of tourism development efforts so as to increase the nation's foreign exchange earnings, mitigation of sound and air pollution in Taipei City.

Expansion of Suao Harbor:

Suao Harbor consists of three inlets, namely, Peifangao, Suao and Nanfangao, respectively used as naval, mercantile and fishing ports. After implemention of the expansion project, it will have a capacity for handling 6,500,000 m.t. of freight at its mercantile port. The project will be carried out in three phases, respectively scheduled for 1974-1976, 1977-1978 and 1979-1981. Its benefits will be: Relieving of the traffic congestion at Keelung and Kaohsiung Harbors, and furtherance of the economic development in the I-Lan area.

Kaohsiung Integrated Steel Mill:

The integrated steel mill now under construction at Kaohsiung is designed for an ultimate annual productive capacity of 6,000,000 m.t. The construction work will be carried out in several stages. The first stage was started in 1973. When completed in 1977, the mill will begin operation with an annual productive capacity of 1,500,000 m.t. of crude steel.

Completion of the steel mill project will bring about a change and modernization in the structure of the local iron and steel industry, hasten the growth of related industries, and save large amounts of foreign exchange as a result of import substitution.

Kaohsiung Shipbuilding Yard:

To meet economic development and national defense requirements, a huge shipyard is being constructed in Kaohsiung. It is designed for building 1,000,000-ton supertankers, with all its facilities planned and engineered for this capability.

The construction began in June 1973 and is scheduled for completion in April 1977. When completed, the shipyard will be able to annually build vessels totalling 1,500,000 tons and do repairs of another 2,500,000 tons. By then, the Republic of China will rank among the world's largest ship builders.

Development of Petrochemical Industry:

Embodied in the plan are the so-called upstream and downstream petrochemical projects. The upstream project is for the establishment of Taiwan's third naphtha cracker (the first one being already in production and the second scheduled to begin operation in 1975) in the Linyuan Petrochemical Industries District in Kaohsiung. The new plant will increase the local supply of basic petrochemicals to meet the need for production of petrochemical intermediates by the downstream industries.

Construction of the third cracker is to be carried out in two stages. The first stage of the project began in 1973 and will be completed in 1975. The erection of the plant's second unit, to be undertaken in the second stage of the project, will follow shortly afterwards. Implementation of the downstream projects, which number 40 in all, are expected to be completed in the next few years.

Economic benefits to accrue from the development of the petrochemical industry will be: (a) Value added to be realized from the production of basic petrochemicals will amount to some US$350 million; (b) raw materials will facilitate the development of a host of related industries; (c) investment opportunities in this vast area of development will attract, and therefore make fruitful use of, large amounts of private and foreign capital.

Nuclear Power Plants:

Construction of the first nuclear plant is well under way in northern Taiwan. It will consist of two units, each equipped with a light-water, nuclear reactor for a generating capacity of 636 megawatts. The project began in November 1970, with completion of the twin units scheduled for October 1975 and October 1977 respectively.

To cope with the rapid increase in the Taiwan Power Company's system load and reduce the overall generating cost of the system, a second nuclear power plant is being constructed. It will also have two units, but the capacity of each will be 850 megawatts. Construction of this plant started in 1973, with the completion of its two units scheduled for 1978 and 1979.

In addition to the above, the nation has completed a number of important infrastructure projects over the years. Among these are: Linkou, Shenau and Nanpu Thermal Power Plants; Northern Cross-Island, East-West Cross-Island and Southern Cross-Island Highways; expansion of Keelung, Kaohsiung and Hualien Harbors; Shihmen, Tsengwen and Tachien Dams; Kaohsiung and Taichung Export Processing Zones; and the Ground Stations for Pacific and Indian Ocean Satellite Communications.

INNOVATIONS IN PUBLIC ADMINISTRATION

With a view to continually introducing innovations in public administration, the Administrative Research and Evaluation Commission (AREC) was activated by the Executive Yuan in 1969 to promote research and development activities among government agencies on the one hand and to exercise the functions of administrative control and evaluation on the other.

Administrative research and development:
The Essentials in Research and Development Efforts Pronounced by AREC:

Research and development efforts of each government agency should be confined chiefly to studies on formulation of work plans and guidelines for its activities, ways to make innovations in its workings and to improve its administrative procedures, and measures to better serve the public.

Besides promoting the prosecution of research and development by its own personel, arrangements should be made to cooperate with other government agencies or academic institutes in undertaking specific study projects, so as to benefit from opinions from different sources and also combine theory with practice.

Detailed, workable plans should be laid out for undertaking study projects approved by the Government, for which effective use should be made of all available manpower, material and financial resources.

Progress in research and development efforts should be subject to regular inspection. Each study project must be implemented according to a clearly formed plan, which should not be suspended or altered unless unsurmountable difficulties are encountered or there are strong reasons for its suspension or alteration.

Promotion of Research and Development Activities Among Various Government Agencies:

Items of research undertaken by various government agencies at the instance of AREC totalled 636 during the past three years. Most of these were aimed at improvement of the workings and administrative procedures of the agencies, thus contributing substantially to the nation's continued improvement in public administration.

Over the years, government agencies have attached ever-increasing importance to research and development, as is readily evidenced by the fact that most of them have enlarged their budgets for research and development activities.

Conducting of Special Studies:

In order to benefit from the expertise and opinions of scholars and specialists in the various fields of public administration, they have been invited to attend a number of symposiums for discussion of specific problems with government officials concerned. During the past two years, special studies were made of 62 selected subjects, of which 27 were concerned with ordinary public affairs and 35 had to do with socio-economic development.

"Suit-the-Convenience-of-the-Public" Movement:

To better serve the public, the AREC has conducted studies for streamlining the various administrative procedures as follows:

Simplification of Household Registration and the Procedures for Application for Transcripts Thereof;

Simplification of the Procedures for Tax Assessment and Payment;

Simplification of the Procedures for Application for Construction Licenses;

Simplification of the Procedures for Land Right Registration;

Simplification of the Procedures for Application for Permit to Travel Abroad;

Simplification of the Procedures for Registration of Business and Industrial Concerns;

Streamlining of the Procedures for Handling People's Petitions;

Improvement of the Over-the-Counter Services at the Government Offices;

Simplification of the Procedures for Application for Qualification Certificates.

ADMINISTRATIVE CONTROL AND EVALUATION

Institution of the Control and Evaluation System:

To put a rein on and to raise the work efficiency of the various government agencies, a system of administrative control and evaluation based on the principle underlying the so-called Three-Phase (Planning-Execution-Evaluation) Process and scientific management methods has been instituted by the Executive Yuan, with AREC and the National Science Council charged with the responsibility of its promotion. The AREC has further undertaken the task of making overall planning of the work, which began in September 1969. After carrying through the positive steps of planning, experimentation, training and trial enforcement, the system was finally brought into being and formally put into practice in July 1970. Meanwhile, a book series of 18 volumes dealing with administrative control and evaluation has been published by AREC to introduce pertinent concepts and thereby streamline the workings of the system.

Over the past year, in pursuance of Premier Chiang's instructions for the various agencies to develop self-control capability, improvement has been repeatedly made in the system of administrative control and evaluation, which has now been placed on a solid basis.

Process of Control and Evaluation:

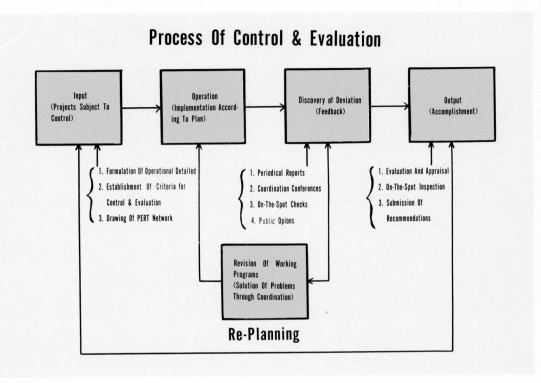

Process Of Control & Evaluation

Input (Projects Subject To Control)

Operation (Implementation According To Plan)

Discovery of Deviation (Feedback)

Output (Accomplishment)

1. Formulation Of Operational Detailed
2. Establishment Of Criteria for Control & Evaluation
3. Drawing Of PERT Network

1. Periodical Reports
2. Coordination Conferences
3. On-The-Spot Checks
4. Public Opions

1. Evaluation And Appraisal
2. On-The-Spot Inspection
3. Submission Of Recommendations

Revision Of Working Programs (Solution Of Problems Through Coordination)

Re-Planning

Tne operational process of the new control and evaluation system is as follows:

Detailed plans are first formulated for each work item or project placed under control, the criteria for control and evaluation are then set up, and subsequently the drawing of PERT network is carried out. With the planning work thus carefully done, the actual operation of the process can then begin.

If, in the course of implementation of the project under control, any deviation or shortfall is discovered from the periodical reports received, discussions held at coordination meetings, on-the-spot checks or the public opinion, coordination measures will then be taken to solve the problems or to urge the agency or agencies concerned to make necessary corrections.

Upon completion of each project subject to control, on-the-spot inspections will be made, with findings and recommendations written into an appraisal report for use as a guide to future project designers.

The accompanying diagram shows the operational process of the control and evaluation system.

Administrative Control at Various Levels of the Government:

In exercising control over the annual work programs of the various government agencies, authority has been delegated to the various levels of the administrative hierarchy by the Executive *Yuan*. Thus, with the exception of the most important items, projects in the annual programs are mostly subject to self-control by the agencies concerned, with performance evaluation undertaken by the authorities at the immediate upper level in each case.

Accordingly, out of a total of 4,504 work items in the annual programs of the various government agencies for the year ended June 30, 1974, only 173 were directly controlled by the Executive *Yuan*, including 66 in the field of general administration, 80 in the field of economic development, and 27 in the field of science advancement.

Follow-Up Checks:

Project evaluation techniques are employed in making follow-up checks with a view to effectively controlling the progress of various work items or projects. Data on the more important projects have been processed by computers, and special attention has all along been given to items that have fallen into arrears in order to unearth the underlying problems and bring about proper solutions by coordinating efforts.

For imposing follow-up checks on matters under special assignment by the heads of the various government agencies and on important resolutions adopted at official meetings, measures prescribed in the "Procedure for Checking-Up of the Execution of Official Business" are to be followed out. Take for instance matters under assignment by Premier Chiang at the Executive Council meetings: there were altogether 472 items for the past two years, out of which 265 were placed under AREC control, with 124 already successfully wound up. The nine major construction projects for acceleration of economic development have all been subjected to follow-up check.

Meanwhile, the various government agencies have been making earnest and gratifying effort at disposal of their work backlogs and at increasing efficiency in document preparation. The habit of procrastinating has been largely rooted out from public offices through the introduction of a series of measures for simplification and expediting paper-work.

Year-End Achievements Appraisal:

Year-end appraisal of the achievements of government agencies and state enterprises has been conducted regularly over the years in accordance with pertinent regulations in force.

In order that this regular practice will not turn into a mere formality of no constructive result, best efforts have been made to apply modern scientific method to the appraisal work and to discover and solve problems through on-the-spot investigations. For instance, in conducting achievements appraisal for the year ended June 30, 1973, a number of problems were brought to light. Recommendations made on the basis of the findings numbered 49 in all – nine on policy matters and 40 concerning state enterprises, with measures subsequently taken by various organizations concerned for finding solution to the problems.

In future, to improve the efficiency in year-end achievement appraisal, the principle of demarcation of responsibilities will be applied. Thus, the work of achievements appraisal will in most cases be entrusted to the authorities having direct jurisdiction over the agency or enterprise concerned. The AREC will only perform the achievements appraisal for those important projects specially assigned to it.

Meanwhile, specialists will be invited to tackle problems arising from serious bottlenecks and dead angles in public administration, with a view to making control and evaluation an increasingly effective means to expedite progress.

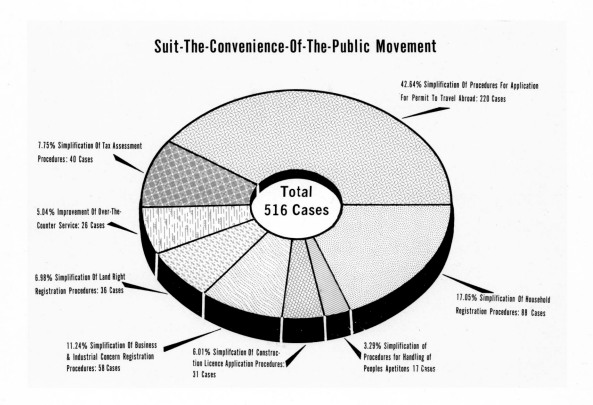

Suit-The-Convenience-Of-The-Public Movement

42.64% Simplification Of Procedures For Application For Permit To Travel Abroad: 220 Cases

7.75% Simplification Of Tax Assessment Procedures: 40 Cases

5.04% Improvement Of Over-The-Counter Service: 26 Cases

6.98% Simplification Of Land Right Registration Procedures: 36 Cases

Total 516 Cases

17.05% Simplification Of Household Registration Procedures: 88 Cases

11.24% Simplification Of Business & Industrial Concern Registration Procedures: 58 Cases

6.01% Simplifcation Of Construction Licence Application Procedures: 31 Cases

3.29% Simplification of Procedures for Handling of Peoples Apetitons 17 Cases

IMPROVEMENT OF LIVING STANDARD

Advancement of social welfare has been especially stressed in the administrative programs of almost all democratic nations of the world today. In the case of the Republic of China, improvement of the livelihood and living standard of the people has been the prime objective of the Government, which is founded on the Principle of the Three People's Principles. Described below are the changes in respect to clothing, food, housing, transportation, and education and recreation in Taiwan in recent years:

CLOTHING:

Taiwan had to import all the clothing materials it needed in the early postwar years. It was through government encouragement and assistance that the textile industry began to grow in the later years. By 1954, for the first time there was a surplus of cotton textiles available for export, although production of man-made fiber had not yet started. In 1961, per capita consumption of cotton fabrics was 17.97 meters, that of woolen textiles, 0.14 meter, and that of man-made fiber fabrics, 1.27 meters. These increased to 52.50 meters, 0.65 meters and 18.08 meters respectively in 1973. (Statistics on consumption of silk, linen and other non-cotton natural fibers are not available.) In sharp contrast with those olden days when the people's clothing was made principally with cotton fabrics which had to be procured from abroad, Taiwan now produces all kinds of textiles and an ever-increasing amount of the products are being exported. Woolens, hemp, and blended fiber fabrics have increased their importance as clothing materials of the people on Taiwan in recent years.

FOOD:

Computations of caloric intake of the people of Taiwan based on the statistics on consumption of 42 kinds of major food items showed that per capita per day average to be 2,430 calories in 1961 and 2,741 calories in 1973, Of the 1961 figure, 1,755 calories or 72.22% were obtained from grain foods and 675 calories or 27.78% from other food items. Of the 1973 figure, 1,637 calories or 59.73% were from grain foods, and 1,104 calories or 40.27% from other food items. The caloric intake required for the human beings varies in amount with the climate of the place they live in. By the applicable standard. Taiwan is standing on a fairly high level.

The protein intake of the people on Taiwan rose from 60.34 grams in 1961 to 72.81 grams in 1973.

HOUSING:

To improve the living conditions of the burgeoning population, the Government has over the years encouraged private investments in housing projects and also undertaken the construction of low-cost housing units for sale to the people on installment plan. Back in 1961, privately owned housing totalled 27,673,212 *ping* (including 640,457 *ping* reinforced concrete structures, 6,615,356 *ping* wooden houses, 9,599,514 *ping* brick-and-stone work, 8,452,198 *ping* earthern constructions and 2,365,687 *ping* bamboo structures). By 1973, the total housing area rose to 57,423,421 *ping* (including 24,755,247 *ping* reinforced concrete structures, 6,590,156 *ping* wooden houses, 14,708,961 *ping* brick-and-stone work, 7,391,-899 *ping* earthern constructions and 3,977,158 *ping* bamboo structures). Increasing percentage of the new houses has been built according to modern construction standards, with reinforced concrete structures increasing the fastest among various categories of construction.

The per capita share in the total housing area rose from 2.48 *ping* in 1961 to 3.69 *ping* in 1973, an increase of 50 %.

TRANSPORTATION:

Besides the development of railway and highway transportation and aviation and shipping reviewed in the Chapter on transportation, the growth in the number of automobiles and motorcycles in use also clearly shows that the life on Taiwan in this aspect has been significantly improved.

Automobiles in use increased from 12,568 in 1961 to 105,278 in 1973, and motorcycles in use, from 32,733 in 1961 to 1,173,015 in 1973, up by 740% and 3,480% respectively. Meanwhile, steady efforts have been made to improve the road conditions, with the entire highway network now composed of high grade paved (asphalt surfaced) roads. In respect to road transport facilities, Taiwan now bears comparison with most other places in the world.

YOUTH ACTIVITIES:

To help promote the physical and intellectual development of the young people, summer and winter vacation recreational programs have been conducted every year since 1953. Students at various levels of schools have benefited from this type of extra-curricular activities. Participants increased from 13,358 (8,365 and 4,993 taking part in the summer and winter camps respectively) in 1953 to 930,269 (532,822 and 397,447 taking part in the summer and winter camps respectively) in 1973. A total of 3,658,211 young men and women (2,236,822 in the summers and 1,421,389 in the winters) had participated in the activities up to the end of 1973.

RECREATION:

To provide the people with amenities of life has also been a serious undertaking of the Government. Thus, in addition to promoting tourism and vacationing activities, recreation in various other proper pastimes has further been actively encouraged by the authorities.

Two pertinent indicators of the recreation activities of the people on Taiwan are the numbers of TV sets and amusement places: In 1973, there were altogether 900,646 TV sets in use, and cinemas, music halls and dancing troupes totalled 815. Revenue from amusement tax during the year amounted to NT$ 222,750,000.

IMPROVEMENT OF LIVING STANDARD

Expenditures By The Private Sector

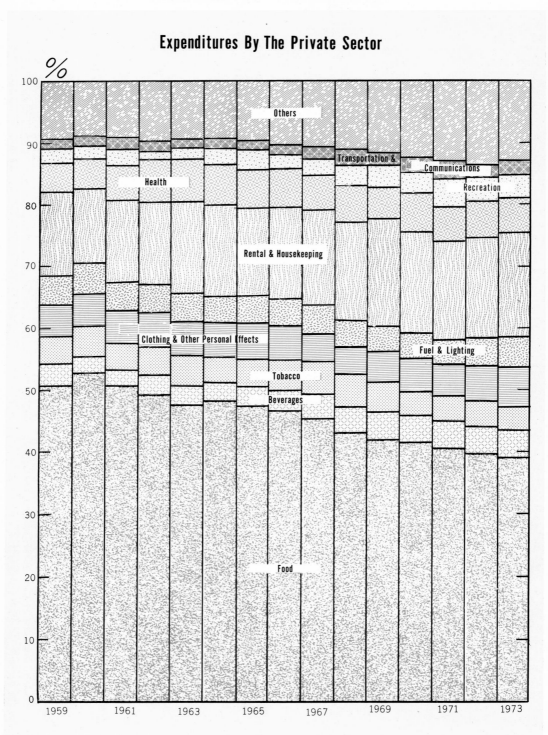